RECLAIMING CHRISTIAN EDUCATION

W9-BGK-666

RECLAIMING CHRISTIAN EDUCATION

FRANCES W. EASTMAN
AND
CAROLYN E. GODDARD

Copyright © 1976 by United Church Press
All Rights Reserved

No part of this publication may be reproduced, stored in a re-
trieval system, or transmitted in any form or by any means, elec-
tronic, mechanical, photocopying, recording or otherwise, without
the prior permission of the publisher, except in the case of
suggestions for research and charts, which may be reproduced
only for specified use and not for sale.

Acknowledgment and appreciation are expressed to the many
local church congregations, pastors, educational leaders in congregations, and numerous other persons committed to the Christian Education Ministry who have contributed reports of congregational programs or have commented on this manuscript. Without
their gracious sharing of experience and time this book could not
have been written.

This book is published by United Church Press for the Division of
Evangelism, Church Extension and Education of The United
Church Board for Homeland Ministries.

All scripture quotations are from the *Revised Standard Version of
the Bible,* copyrighted 1946 and 1952 by the Division of Christian
Education, National Council of Churches, and are used by permission.

Library of Congress Cataloging in Publication Data
Eastman, Frances W
     Reclaiming Christian education.

     "Published by United Church Press for the Division of
Evangelism, Church Extension, and Education of the United
Church Board for Homeland Ministries."
     1. Christian education.   I. Goddard, Carolyn E., 1918-
joint author.   II. United Church Board for Homeland Minis-
tries.   Division of Evangelism, Church Extension, and Educa-
tion.   III. Title.
BV1471.2.E2   268   76-26927
ISBN 0-8298-0323-8 pbk.

United Church Press
1505 Race Street
Philadelphia, Pennsylvania 19102

CONTENTS

CHAPTER 1

WHERE IS CHRISTIAN EDUCATION IN THE CHURCH TODAY?

What is the church today? What it has always been: the church is "us"—you and I and the people all over the world who call themselves Christian, who gather to worship God and learn of the faith and live out that faith. The church of today is the product of the working of God in the people who have gone before us. Beginning with the apostles, people expressed their commitment to Christ by preaching, teaching, and reaching out to others. One generation shared the faith with the next. That generation made the faith its own and in turn passed it on to the next. Forms of passing on the faith changed from time to time to fit people's needs and current ways of teaching, preaching, and reaching out to the world. But passing on the faith has always been a generation-to-generation sharing process. Because of it, the church has been a living force for twenty centuries.

For many years Christian education, or education in the church, has been one of the important ways in which the faith has been passed from one generation to the next. In recent decades this education has taken a variety of forms, especially classes organized for various age groups from young to old. The name most familiar for this structured kind of planned education is "Sunday school" or "church school." Committed superintendents, teachers, and other leaders have helped to share the faith with many generations through this work.

The purpose of this book is to suggest what and how churches can contribute to the growth, life and mission of the church today and tomorrow through Christian education ministries that meet the opportunities and the challenges of the 1970s and beyond.

WHAT IS CHRISTIAN EDUCATION?

If asked that question, some church members may respond with reflections of their own childhood experiences: "The Sunday school" . . . "Something for the children" . . . "Teaching the Bible."

Others may reply out of different experiences: "Something that will help me understand the Christian faith" . . . "Helping children and young people become Christians."

Still other people might add: "A program that will interest young people and keep them in the church or bring them into it."

All these responses contain elements of Christian education, but they do not encompass the whole of it. They are not complete answers for sharing the faith with others in the 1970s. What has been done educationally in the past needs to be examined in the light of the needs of today. Otherwise our educational ministries are likely to be inadequate or unsuited to the present.

Through Christian education that is adequate for today the church must equip and enable persons (individuals, families, the whole congregation)—

- to make the faith and heritage of the Christian community their own;
- to continue to grow in Christian commitment;
- and to participate in God's continuing work of making the good news of love, justice, and well-being a reality for all humankind within the life of persons, homes, congregations, community, nation, and the whole world.

CHALLENGE!

For many years Christian education in the form of the church school has been the primary way of sharing the faith and passing it on to the next generation. But in many churches at present the church school is said to be in trouble. Fewer students are enrolled than ten or twenty years ago. Interest is declining.

Does this mean that Christian education is fading away? Or the church? NO! It means that a new challenge to Christian education confronts us. Closer examination of the educational ministry of many churches discloses that ways of carrying on education are changing along with the rapid change in other aspects of our culture. New forms of doing church school education are emerging in many churches. Additional places and times in the congregation's life are being used to offer exciting education for people of all ages. Christian education is being reclaimed and reshaped so that we can more effectively share the faith in today's world. All churches need to think more broadly, more deeply, more imaginatively about what Christian education is and how it occurs. That is the challenge for the present and for the future.

CHAPTER 2

LOOKING AT CHRISTIAN EDUCATION WHOLE

Adam, age 3½, is involved in the life and worship of the church as he attends the nursery school, beats rhythms for the junior choir, dashes around among people during the coffee hour, and participates in festivals with the entire church family. Through these activities Adam is learning about the church, and what it means to be a part of this community of faith.

Debbie, age 13, finds church a busy, happy place. She sings in the senior choir, is a member of the confirmation class, participates in the youth group, and with her family shares in all-church activities. She takes her turn in helping with church suppers, and plays her recorder to help group singing. Debbie is getting well-acquainted with many Christian adults in her church and is growing in her knowledge and understanding of the Christian faith. When she seeks confirmation, she will be able to make a meaningful commitment to Christ and his church.

Peggy, mother of four, recently divorced, needed a group of people who would give her and her family friendship and support. She searched among several groups in her town, and found that Hillside Church offered what she needed. Other parents with similar problems were among the members of an adult class that really shared issues of faith and life. Fellowship suppers and seasonal festivals gave Peggy a chance to use her artistic talents. In time she was elected to one of the church boards. As her children participated in church school, Sunday worship, suppers and festivals, youth events and family cluster gatherings, they too discovered that the church was their "extended family." Peggy considers herself and her children fortunate to be part of a church where there are so many ways of learning what it means to be a Christian today.

Jonas found himself faced with a difficult decision when retirement came. His job had kept him for years in a metropolitan area, but since his wife's death, four years earlier, he had become lonelier and lonelier. Life in the city had lost its appeal for him, so he moved to a small community, several states distant, where a good many retired people lived. Jonas went to the community church as his first place to try to enter into a new life. People were cordial, somewhat to his surprise. Being asked home for Sunday dinner by a deacon made Jonas happier than he had been for some time. It wasn't long before other church members invited him to share in trips to nearby historic sites. Taking short trips seemed to be a favorite community enterprise, especially for the friends Jonas made as he became involved in other activities: a craft center, and leading book-and-talk sessions at the local nursing home. Eventually Jonas was encouraged to try out—and play—a leading role in the community theater. For Jonas, the church proved an open doorway to a new, invigorating life in both church and community. In the process, he found himself becoming much interested in learning more about the faith.

Gerald and Lucy always went to church. At least, they were both present except when Gerald's busy medical practice kept him away on Sunday morning. When that happened, Lucy went by herself. She liked the fellowship, and somehow—although she had a hard time putting it into words—she felt a tug inside herself, "as though a power outside me was trying to talk to me," as she was able to express it to Gerald. She particularly felt this way during sermons when the minister linked the meaning of Christian faith with day-to-day problems of living. A similar feeling also occasionally came when one of the deacons read the scripture and included helpful comments on the passage's setting in the biblical story and the significance of the passage.

The sense of being spoken to did not leave Lucy. She began to wonder: What is this all about? Can this be God speaking to me—that's a phrase the minister uses sometimes. If it is God trying to get through to me, what am I supposed to think or do?

Lucy's puzzlement suddenly reached a climax and a sense of direction one Sunday morning. Gerald was at church with her. "A Moment of Concern" talk pointed out several serious community situations and called for personal action by church members. Disastrous living conditions for the elderly, excessive rent raises and elimination of services to tenants in apartment houses, the closing down of day care centers, and pollution threats to the city water system were mentioned as evils facing the city and the entire county. "Christians need to take a stand and work on these issues to make changes in the system that permits them."

Lucy felt something burst inside her. "Yes! Yes!" she said to herself. "I could work on things like that. I have time, and they need to have something done about them." To the minister after the service she said, "This morning I got a new vision of what a Christian can do. How do I go about helping to do something to change those unjust situations?"

Talks with the minister and Gerald led Lucy to volunteer service on several investigative committees in the community. "Justice" and "compassionate action" became religious terms for her. She felt more alive, and rejoiced that she and Gerald shared the same concern for faith and action. Lucy became more and more active, always trying to test her stands against what she was increasingly hearing and thinking about in her church life.

Eventually Lucy gathered courage to run for membership on the County Council in the area where she lived. It was the legislative body that could vote changes in the system. She had never dreamed of doing such a thing, but, "maybe this is my Amos bit," she would say. When she won election, no one was more surprised than she. "Could I say that I've heard what God was trying to say to me?" she asked Gerald. "Our pastor says I've been thinking theologically, and action has resulted. I've never used that term before, but if that's what's been happening, fine. What a tremendous change in my life—our lives—all this has brought! And maybe in the community too!"

The eighth-grade class had long made a name for itself in Second Church. Membership had been fairly constant for years, about six boys and five girls, every one of them lively, and several of them talented. Bob and Macon both played the trumpet and were in demand for every Christmas and Easter service. Laurene was close to being a violin prodigy, and frequently played obbligatos for the choir or special Sunday solos. Helene, assisted by her mother, often baked the loaf of bread for the monthly service of Holy Communion. Others were members of the youth choir or helped out with ushering. Most of the class attended services as well as church school. Among themselves they would argue about conditions at school, in the town, or in the church.

Then came time for confirmation class. They all joined the class, pledging with the minister to fulfill certain obligations in weekly study sessions, a monthly retreat, a service project, and creation of their own statements of faith. The final decision "to join or not to join" would be one for each young person to make.

During the year of confirmation study, the eighth-graders began to feel as though they were putting together jigsaw puzzle pieces. Bible stories, church history, other information and ideas were recalled from their church school studies. Bits of information gleaned from sermons, the kinds of relationships they had made with other church members, hymns and anthems learned in choir, all began to come together to help them understand faith more clearly for themselves. A sense of "This is what the church is all about" began to come clear as they progressed through the year of confirmation study. When they shared their statements of faith with the church officers, and each announced her or his decision about joining the church, all the pieces of the puzzle seemed to fall in place, as Macon put it. "This was a year of tough work, but it sure pulled together all these things I've experienced in church," he said.

At a weekend retreat held at Central Church one fall, the participants ranged in age from young people to adults. Several people found that they were deeply concerned with the meaning of faith and prayer, and how genuine devotional activities affect the way people live and what they are able to do. This group of four got deeply immersed in talking among themselves about prayer and personal spiritual life. Praying together brought them to commit themselves to meet twice a month for a prayer circle and to share devotional reading and personal experiences that had occurred in the days between meetings. "Worship and taking part in other church activities have helped us see that we need this to let God shape our lives and our work," they said. "Without this retreat we might never have been led to this new vision and commitment."

WHAT IS "WHOLISTIC"?

Through education ministries, the church wants to help people learn—whether as individual persons, families, special groups, or the congregation as a whole. These examples show that Christian education occurs in all aspects of the church's life. Some learning is the result of planned educational opportunities; some results from experiences planned for other purposes; and some from unplanned experiences or personal relationships. The latter two kinds of learning might be described as educational by-products of church life and events. The whole life of a congregation offers times and places in which Christian learning and Christian educa-

14

tion may occur. This is what is meant when the word WHOLISTIC is used in relation to Christian education. Whether spelled with or without "w" (wholistic or holistic), the reference to Christian education is the same: a broad-visioned approach aimed at discovering and developing the many ways that education and learning can occur in the life of a church and parish. The whole church offers opportunities for Christian education and learning.

In developing educational ministries that are responsive to the wholistic approach, educational leaders need to investigate several of the "Whats" and "Hows" that make up its ingredients or elements. This book deals with these elements. In the remaining pages we will be taking a closer look at each. Each reader should keep his or her own church's life clearly in mind during this examining process. For a wholistic vision and approach to education in the church to emerge with all its exciting possibilities, the "Whats" and "Hows" need to be pictured specifically in terms of one's own local church.

CHAPTER 3

WHAT MAKES UP THE WHOLE?

1. PEOPLE

To reclaim and reshape the church's educational ministry we start with people and we end with people, in contrast to making creeds and their acceptance the primary focus. Sharing the faith from generation to generation is a "people process." In this people process, all the people are learners. At the same time they are also sharers. Knowing just who is in a congregation is important. Ways of doing this will be discussed on pages 89-92. But first of all, we should remember that each person in the people process is a human being with distinctive personality, gifts, needs, and abilities. Most congregations will probably include, in varying numbers, infants, children, youth, young adults, middle adults, senior citizens, the very elderly, and the housebound or ill. Even the smallest church will probably have representatives of most of this cross section of people.

Whoever they are, or however many or few there are, the people will include male and female. They may live in various relationships: as single persons, friends sharing an apartment, couples, families with one or two parents and one or more children, residents of a retirement center or a nursing home. They may differ in backgrounds of family life, early upbringing, schooling, personal experiences in the world, vocation or occupation. Goals and ambitions may be infinitely varied too, and different for every individual. Each of these people needs to know and share in God's love and the joy of commitment to Jesus Christ.

Because in the people process of sharing faith from generation to generation, people of all ages need to be involved in the sharing process or touched by it, education in the church has a tremendous responsibility for doing its share in making the people process vital, alive, and responsive to persons.

Learning occurs as people receive new information or new insights, undergo changes in feelings or attitudes, make new decisions, take new actions, think about what they are doing and why. Sharing takes place as people exchange ideas and feelings, express their understandings of the faith, disclose their questions and interests and desires, and live out their commitments according to where they are in relation to the faith at any time.

This people process can also be called a teaching-and-learning process, in which people are both teachers and learners, even though they often may be designated one or the other in a given educational situation in the church. Even in planned educational events, people teach each other and learn from each other in addition to being taught by the designated teacher or leader (who is also a learner!). In learning-center groups, for example, older children often help younger children with everything from locating places on Bible maps to making macrame worship hangings, while the teachers serve as enablers by helping other children search for biblical passages on the session's theme, telling a story, or sharing a tape in order to enlarge the student's understanding and involvement in the concerns of the session.

What are some of the things that people do in the life of the whole congregation that play a part in the people process? Here are a few. The preacher preaches—what, and how he or she does so, are important. So are what and how teachers teach. Attitudes shown by ushers and church officers communicate. The kinds of decisions made by boards and committees reveal their commitment and values. Budget priorities that are chosen tell what the congregation thinks is really important. How the congregation serves the world's needs and those of its members discloses whether the people really care.

These are only a few "for instances" of the "people process." Everything people of the congregation do expresses what the faith means to them and what their commitment to others is, whether inside or outside the church, and whether they are aware of it or not.

In the theological words often used in speaking of Christian faith, Jesus Christ is called the Incarnation—the presence of God in a human being. The faith has been, and still is, shared by our incarnation of it in all that we do.

2. HERITAGE OF THE FAITH

Each new generation needs to hear the Christian story, participate in it, and make it its own. And every present generation needs to continue to grow in understanding of and commitment to the heritage. In the wholistic approach to Christian education, our entire heritage must be shared and studied by both present and future members of the church.

What, essentially, is the heritage? Christians believe that God has been, still is, and will continue to be at work in human history and in human lives. The heart of the Christian heritage is the good news of Jesus Christ in whom God and God's purposes are most fully made known to human beings. In Jesus of Nazareth, the Christ, God entered our human condition, loved, taught, and called all people to love God and their fellow human beings so that salvation might come to all. Through Christ's death and resurrection, we know that God is still with us, calling us to join in these purposes for all humankind. God's Holy Spirit is at work among us. The heritage has found expression in many different forms. It continues to be newly expressed as each generation or culture interprets the faith in the light of its own special experiences.

The biblical story of God's action and people's response to it is our primary source of the heritage. Bible study, therefore, is basic in Christian education. It is a never-completed activity. We need to explore its riches throughout our lives.

Young children learn to know God and God's love through relationships with Christians who love and accept them, and forgive them when they do wrong. The children also hear stories and passages from the Bible itself. These are carefully selected according to the child's ability to understand and appreciate the Bible and to arouse his or her interest in learning more of the story of God's love. Children become familiar with Jesus as a very special person who showed God's love for people.

As they grow older, children become familiar with many persons and events of the Bible, and discover more of God's ways for us today by studying God's work in Bible times. They begin to explore the special meaning of Jesus Christ, the Son of God. Deepening and enriching exploration of biblical content continues into youth and adult years as people examine our story more fully and wrestle with its meaning and what it says for life today.

The heritage also has been, and continues to be, expressed and interpreted through people, events, and modes of communication. The history of the church through twenty centuries, and the story of a worldwide church at work today, are a continuation of the story of the people of the Bible, for we belong to this people whom God calls to join in mission.

Through the centuries the continuing story of God's work has been recorded in creeds, meditations, poetry, and prayer that express convictions, intercessions, and spiritual pilgrimages. Painting, sculpture, the dance, stained glass and architecture—from cathedrals to simple church meeting houses—have told the story in visual form. Hymns and other music, worship and celebration, motion pictures and television specials bear testimony to the faith that has moved many peoples and influenced the history of the world.

Various church movements have also sought to express Christian commitment in ways that best responded to cultural and social demands of their time: monastic living, communal societies, spiritual renewal groups, action for justice and liberation of peoples and systems in the social order, the missionary effort to carry the good news to all parts of the world.

All this heritage is part of the "stuff" of Christian education. Sometimes with a touch of glory, sometimes with the pall of tragedy, human beings have expressed and continue to live out, preach and teach the good news made known to us in Jesus Christ.

Just as our heritage has been expressed in many ways, so it is shared, learned, and made part of a person's life in a variety of church experiences and activities, both planned teaching/learning events and learnings inherent in other activities in the church's life. Examples are:

- the church school and study groups for all ages, by age and by intergenerational groupings;
- preparation for confirmation and receiving of other new members;
- worship and celebration services;
- choir and other art groups;
- preaching and hearing sermons;
- meetings of boards, committees and other official organizations;
- the atmosphere of the building itself;
- the observation of the great faith seasons of the church year (Christmas, Easter, Pentecost);
- fellowship and informal or specially planned events;
- relationships of persons with each other;
- the congregation's outreach into the community and the wider world.

Keep such a varied array of possibilities for sharing the heritage in mind as this book is read—and note others that you think of in your own church situation. Doing so will help the wholistic vision and approach to the church's educational ministry become real to you.

3. MISSION

God's call is still the same one that Jesus gave to his first followers: Follow me. Tell the good news of God's love in every part of the world. Live lives that care for others. Serve your neighbors' needs for justice, liberation, and fullness of life.

The mission proclaimed in the New Testament is still the church's mission. To help people of all ages understand this mission, commit themselves to it, and find specific ways of participating in it, is Christian education's major responsibility in the church.

Mission is more than designing a sharing project or giving money, although it may well include both. Mission is the whole set of personal convictions, attitudes and actions that reveal how one thinks and feels about the entire world, from one's family and neighborhood to the most distant peoples. Mission is expression of the desire that everyone "may have life and have it more abundantly." Christians and churches everywhere are involved in mission as they take various actions to share God's love with others.

Paul is often called the first missionary. From its beginning in Jerusalem, he took the good news of God's love in Christ to the Mediterranean world. In the centuries that followed, Christians have carried the good news to all parts of the world. Evangelists, doctors, teachers, farmers, specialists in many fields of work who were committed to use their talents in Christ's service have been among the bearers. Christianity came to the United States and this entire hemisphere, from Europe and Asia, brought by many groups from many lands.

Thus mission moves from others to us, from us to others, at home or beyond our own borders. Christians in countries all over the world now participate in mission, both within their own lands and by sending persons and support to mission in other countries. Although we sometimes do not realize it, in the United States we are on the receiving as well as the giving end of mission. For example, pastors and their families from Japan and the Philippines, Europe and Africa, have come to share their faith with us.

They serve as resident pastors in conferences or associations. Or they teach at theological schools. And churches from other countries have sent help for American disaster victims—as when, a few years ago, Japanese churches sent a shipload of food to hungry, unemployed people in Seattle.

Workers from the United States now go at the request of churches in other countries to serve under their direction. "Overseas" mission work is now a two-way process.

And, of course, as individual Christians we engage in mission right where we are—in various places, and in a variety of ways.

To share in mission we must first know the faith story and respond to it. Then we can participate in mission in ways that open up to us. We can make changes in our own living practices that will help to free needed foods and other resources for distribution in places of need. We can help children and young people develop understanding and respect for the cultures of other peoples. The same is true for adults. We can spread the good news to people in our own communities and invite them into our church fellowship or serve their needs in a variety of ways. We can learn how to work to improve public policy so there will be greater justice in distributing the world's resources, and we can help others learn to do so too. By sending workers and giving money we can provide assistance to churches in all parts of the world to train their own leaders. We can gain new understanding of what it means to be Christian from missionaries sent by other countries to our own. We can make sharing in the wider work of the church a budget priority by designating funds for a variety of world-church endeavors. These are examples of the kinds of activities and learnings that can go on in many parts of the congregation's life. They teach what God's mission is for us in our time and how we can participate in it. Such experiences, where they occur in the life of the church, are education in mission.

As education in mission takes place in our churches it can help everyone discover more fully the meaning of oneness in Christ: that all human beings are brothers and sisters and that we live in one world. We have been teaching these Christian truths for years as religious convictions. In the 1970s they have also become economic and social realities. The interdependence of nations and the effects of this have to be taken into account in our day-to-day lives. The vast differences in living conditions around the world have become more clearly visible. So have those at home.

Hunger and famine afflict every nation, in varying degrees. The rich seem to gain control of property and influence at a faster pace in many countries, while the poor become poorer, unemployment rises, and housing declines. We can no longer ignore the unequal distribution and use of the world's resources between the "have" and the "have not" nations and peoples. Mass communications and technology have made us all, sometimes terrifyingly, close neighbors. We are finding that we do not know or understand, or sometimes even like, the cultures and goals of some of our brothers and sisters in other parts of the world. But we are discovering that we must live in close contact, sharing with each other in many of life's essentials, and growing in appreciation and understanding.

One task of Christian mission in the local church is to help everyone to understand the implications, for life today and the future, of the Christian conviction of oneness in Christ. Learning more about people and life in other parts of the world, and facing up to how we relate to them and act toward them on many levels of life, is an essential part of helping people of all ages to participate in mission.

As we reclaim Christian education, we must include involvement in the changing ways of learning about, and taking part in, Christian mission.

4. CONGREGATIONAL LIFE

We have seen that sharing the faith from generation to generation does not occur in a vacuum. It occurs as people participate in the life, work, and mission of the church. Some people think of the church as a collection of organizations and scheduled events—an arrangement of building blocks, so to speak. But in reality a congregation that is alive is much more like a human body. The Apostle Paul speaks of the church that way in 1 Corinthians 12, and another name for the church has always been "the body of Christ." A human body is a system of interrelated parts that affect each other in their functioning. When one part is out of order, the entire body (or person) is not up to par. What happens to the nerves affects all the rest of the body. So it goes.

In a similar manner, what happens in one part of the congregation's life affects members and their participation in the life, work and mission of the church. Sometimes the effects of actions or events are affirmative; sometimes negative. Congregational life in any of its parts can touch the whole congregation and has an effect on attitudes, faith commitments, and participation. As we have noted before, the whole church—or any part of its life—teaches. Let's take a look at two real-life church situations and what they taught. Names have been changed, but not the realities of what happened.

Here is Church Number One. St. Peter's, as we will call it, 1,100 members, faced a financial crisis. The church building needed a roof and several other major repairs. The cost estimate for the repairs was $40,000. The regular budget could not possibly provide that amount. Just as the church council was ready to propose a building fund campaign, the denomination, in a national relief drive, asked St. Peter's to pledge as its share $10,000 a year for three years for a campaign to work on world hunger and other world human crises. The council called a congregational meeting and presented the need for $40,000 and the request for the three-year pledge of $30,000. A heated debate followed. Finally the congregation voted to raise the $40,000 for building repairs, and to postpone considering any commitment to the world hunger campaign.

By its action, St. Peter's effectively taught children and young people—and some adults too—that the congregation does *not* love its neighbor as itself. As children hear parents discuss the decision, church school lessons about the second part of the Great Commandment won't mean much at St. Peter's and young people's cynicisms about adults' double standards of what they say and what they do are reinforced. The congregational life, or one of its actions, was a potent negative sharing of the faith.

Variations of this example can be found in almost every church. Take Church Number Two, Bethel Church, 230 members. It was formed by the merger of two smaller congregations, each of which was finding it tough going alone. Controversy arose between the two churches over which building to use, so both were sold and a small new building erected. "Our new building" was a source of pride to all. One of the former congregations, however, had an old but good pipe organ which it wanted to put in the new building. To fix up and install the organ would cost about $1,000. Members of the second congregation did not want something "old" from the other congregation to be installed in the new building. They successfully blocked the raising of the $1,000. After this controversial start for a new life together, teaching the words of Jesus to "Love one another as I have loved you," or the Golden Rule, might well seem an academic exercise to many. Meanwhile, the organ remains stored in the barn of one of the church members.

These are examples of negative teaching via decisions and events in the congregational life. Fortunately, they are in a minority compared to the positive teachings found in every church.

At the other extreme from the above examples, there are churches that have mortgaged their buildings to raise money to build low-income housing, or to provide capital for the establishment of minority group businesses. Almost every church has a "Martha" who visits sick and shut-ins, calls on new people in the community, and finds numerous ways to share the joy of her faith. There are ushers and greeters whose genuinely friendly welcome reminds everyone, especially the newcomer, of the description of the early followers of Jesus: "Behold, how these Christians love one another." Every church has people who generously share with the church their talents of music, teaching, gardening, room decoration, business management, and the like, as an expression of thanksgiving to God. Through their sharing, others learn what it means to be a committed Christian.

Living expressions of faith like these create an atmosphere of love, an environment of community welcome, and communicate the sense that life in this congregation has the distinctive character of being Christians who care for one other. Experiencing this special character of a congregation's life through participation in specific planned events—or as the by-products we mentioned earlier—may help to change people's emotions, incentives, and relationships. Such experiences may also affect what people do—their actions, behavior, purposes in life, choices and decisions, just as the corporate acts of St. Peter's and Bethel Churches had their effects. *Changing thinking, feeling, intentions, and actions is one way to describe what learning and teaching are all about.*

Because the life of a congregation provides so many places and situations where teaching and learning can go on, educational ministry developed from a wholistic point of view must take into account the learnings that are occurring. It must offer a variety of teaching/learning opportunities that will help persons grow in their understanding of, and commitment to, Jesus Christ and God's mission.

CHAPTER 4

ELEMENTS TO BE CONSIDERED: BASIC ASSUMPTIONS

1. DECIDE WHAT WE WANT CHRISTIAN EDUCATION TO ACCOMPLISH AND WHERE IT CAN OCCUR

Many churches take for granted that there must be a Christian education program in the church. There always has been one. Naturally, people say, there should continue to be one. The board of education, or a steering committee, takes responsibility and works hard at setting up church school, youth groups, perhaps adult Bible or other study groups, and similar opportunities for carrying on education. Resources are chosen from denominational recommendations, or other sources that the leaders like. The program goes on through the year, with perhaps a special program given for the entire congregation to show what has been done, particularly in the church school and youth group. Few, if any, people ask just why this work is being done.

A similar process goes on the next year, and the next. Criticisms may arise; leaders may be hard to enlist. But Christian education is an established program of the church and is carried on almost as a separate building block in the structure of the church's organizations.

Almost no one asks, "What are we trying to accomplish through Christian education in this church?" Yet that question should be asked by every church. Without it, opportunities for evaluating and improving are likely to be passed by. Christian education is not just a "thing" to carry on. It is a means of accomplishing a purpose, a long-range goal or accomplishment that will equip persons to share in, and contribute to, the growth, life and mission of the church today and tomorrow.

KNOWING THE CHURCH'S PURPOSES
A general purpose for Christian education, however, should not exist all by itself. It needs to be made specific in relation to sev-

eral other foundations of the church's life. This should be done in terms of each congregation's particular approach to its life and mission, the congregation's particular understanding of its style and reason for being, and the congregation's long-range purposes. What is to be accomplished through Christian education must also be decided in the light of the church's beliefs about theology (pages 41-54) and Christian education (pages 54-87). It must be integrally related to the church's constitution or other basic statement of the overall purposes and goals of the church.

A pastor who takes seriously his call to be a teaching as well as preaching minister was recently asked to fill out a questionnaire about education in the congregation. The questionnaire phrased questions in terms of a wholistic approach to local church education. Replies by this pastor were thoughtful and honest. At the end of his answers, he wrote: "This questionnaire is very good for me as it makes me realize how unthought-out our educational program is in terms of linkage with our church constitution. We are presently in the process of revising our constitution and the examination of the whole document by the congregation gives us a natural lead-in to making some conscious linkages."

THE CHURCH'S LONG-RANGE GOALS

The first step in deciding what we want to accomplish through education in the church, then, is to be aware of what the church's long-range goals are. Here are a few samples of church goals. Each is different from the other, but note how each reflects the church's understanding of itself and of its mission as the church believes God calls this congregation to carry it out.

A CHURCH IN NEW JERSEY. This church went through an extended process of goal-setting. The following statement was developed and approved by the Executive Board as an outgrowth of that process and as a preliminary step toward measurable goals for each board to undertake.

1. This church welcomes all who are searching for the truth and will endeavor to provide a religious home for a wide spectrum of belief.
2. This church is willing to experiment with new forms of worship, education, and service, in order to communicate the Christian faith to a generation deeply immersed in social change, religious freedom, and theological growth.

28

3. This church seeks to provide opportunities for deep personal interaction so that we may find personal fulfillment through discovery of our true selves and each other.
4. This church seeks to provide a ministry that honors and assists individuals, couples, and families as they seek to cope with their personal circumstances and inner conflicts.
5. This church, in the spirit expressed above, encourages participation in the social development of our communities.
6. This church seeks to provide a sense of belonging, fellowship and personal involvement among all its members.

The second item in this goal statement specifies education as a major means of communicating the faith. Note that the statement indicates willingness to seek new ways and forms, and also gives a picture of concerns of the parishioners. Other parts of this general goal statement suggest possible areas of content and types of methods that might be used in providing education that is in keeping with the spirit and self-understanding of the church and how it is to carry out mission. A thoughtful board of Christian education would find in this statement many points to consider as it works on specific ways in which Christian education can help to fulfill the church's goals and be a part of the whole life of the congregation.

A CHURCH IN IOWA. At a planning conference, the congregation of this church studied carefully the Statement of Faith of the United Church of Christ, the denomination to which the church belongs. After thoughtful consideration the following covenant was adopted as the "PURPOSE OF THE CONGREGATION":

Having accepted the Statement of Faith, the members of this congregation will endeavor to be a fellowship which will strengthen the Christian way of life in our community and throughout the world through worship, stewardship, education, and service, and to provide an atmosphere for personal growth and commitment.

This is a brief statement of purpose —but it is comprehensive. By reading it carefully, a board of Christian education can find education mentioned as one major means of accomplishing the congregation's purpose. In addition, there is mention of other specific areas of church life which could be dealt with in an educational program.

TWO CHURCHES IN WISCONSIN. In a Wisconsin city, two churches, one Lutheran and the other a United Church of Christ congregation, share one building as the Christian Community. Worship and the Sacraments are conducted separately, but education, outreach, finances, staff and fellowship are shared. A task force developed the following Statement of Purpose for the United Church congregation:

We are human beings struggling together; creatures of hope and despair, love and hate; we come together as a segment of the world with common hopes and expectations, acknowledging our dependence on God and each other.

We affirm our belief in God and in Jesus the Christ. We believe the living Spirit of God is present as we worship and as we interact with people; it is that Spirit which gives direction to our actions. We recognize Jesus' life as an expression of the potentiality of man and affirm that just as He is, we also are creatures of God. Distinctive marks of our identity include sharing in Christ's baptism and eating at His table.

We affirm the goodness of God's world and our willingness to serve that world as a community. Community is about people. The purpose of this Christian community is to grow limbs for reducing distances, limbs for loving, accepting, forgiving and serving, with each individual choosing his own avenue of expression. Thus we come hearing a call to be a community, a summons out of isolation, an invitation-to-be-with-each-other and to-be-for-each-other.

We come together to seek new understandings and to prepare ourselves for engagement—not to be separated or disengaged from the world but to let the world and life events set our agenda. We wish to be free to-be-for-others and declare that the church is her true self only when she exists for humanity.

This open, person- and faith-concerned statement of purpose for the church would suggest that many aspects of the church's concerns could be integrated with those of the other church in development of the joint education ministry. It also suggests that opportunities for knowing and being part of a community committed to Christ, and for serving and witnessing in the world, will offer many unplanned learning or by-product, experiences. The pastor of the church writes: "Educational goals relating to our church purpose stress: (1) Strong grounding in biblical faith; (2) discovering together what it means to be in a community of people; and (3) how our faith witnesses to the world we find ourselves in."

30

CHRISTIAN EDUCATION PURPOSES AND THE CHURCH'S GOALS

Once a church's overall or long-range goals and purposes are known, *a second step is to decide which goals, or portions of goals, should be fulfilled through Christian education—in whole or in part.*

Christian education cannot do everything in the church, any more than evangelism or stewardship or worship can fulfill completely every need or purpose. But education *can* contribute to many of the goals.

For example, the first item in the New Jersey statement welcomes all who search for truth, and seeks to provide a religious home for a wide spectrum of belief. An educational program could offer planned study opportunities that would take into account a variety of beliefs and concerns. It would also be concerned that church members would be open to listening to and hearing diverse points of view, and to encouraging real dialogue and community of spirit among people who think and feel differently about important concerns. For example, there are many persons to whom partaking of the Lord's Supper in fellowship with others is a time when the presence of the Spirit is deeply experienced. There are others for whom Holy Communion is a peculiar, disquieting experience. Leaders in education could encourage the pastor to use sermons to present the spectrum of beliefs, and could urge diaconates and consistories or church councils to allow time for theological and other study. In the church school and youth groups, the story of the Last Supper and the use of the Eucharist in New Testament times might lead students into study of Holy Communion. Confirmation classes would certainly go deeply into its meaning.

The second statement in the New Jersey church's goal mentions education but suggests experimenting with new forms as a means to the end of communicating the faith to a generation faced with certain needs. This statement offers a specific purpose for education. It also suggests both a style that is open to trying new forms (not the same thing year after year if it is not effective) and suggests three areas of potential concern that will need to be translated into work appropriate to persons of various ages and situations. At the same time, experimentation is for a serious purpose—not just for the joy of doing things differently.

The third statement in this church's goals is concerned with personal growth and fulfillment. Educational ministries can contribute to its accomplishment by being concerned with the quality of relationships (planned or unplanned) between teachers and students in all educational settings because through personal relationships the gospel is communicated and the faith is exemplified. Structured study of the faith will also contribute to this goal, for relationships are equally important here.

The fourth goal emphasizes ministry to all persons in relation to their personal needs and difficulties. Here again, education can contribute by planning educational settings that deal with growth as a Christian. It can help teachers and leaders become skilled in working with learners "where they are" and accepting learners' needs and problems as important teaching/learning content.

Social improvement of communities where church members live is the fifth goal. Here education in the church can contribute both opportunities to learn of social needs, and genuine experiences in participating in community situations through service projects and work for justice and other human concerns.

The last statement is concerned with providing a sense of belonging, fellowship and personal involvement among all members. This is a specific goal for all Christian education work. It is a foundation of teaching and learning, and also a by-product of education which is truly a two-way people process.

The above brief analysis is an illustration of how a board of Christian education might develop its work in relationship to fulfillment of the church's goals through educational ministry. All six church goals offer possibilities for Christian education. Some (two, three, four, and six) offer explicit opportunities and settings for planned education program units. Others present opportunities in which unplanned teaching and learning will go on, but perhaps not in units planned to be primarily educational programs. These unplanned, or by-product, learnings must be taken into account as boards of education look at educational development in the whole life of the congregation. As we have already said, unplanned learnings are often some of the most important learnings in the "people process" of sharing the faith.

EDUCATIONAL PURPOSES MAY REFLECT THE CHURCH'S GOALS

A church in Minnesota developed a statement of parish education purpose based on data taken from responses to questionnaires received from the congregation. This church looks upon the church goals and Christian education goals as being fundamentally the same and education as one means through which members are striving to achieve these goals. Here is the statement of what this church hopes to accomplish:

Our parish education program will be designed to provide opportunities for persons of all ages—

- to grow spiritually as Christians so that the services of worship, the Bible, and the history and teachings of the church will have increased meaning in their lives.
- to become involved in the life of the congregation in ways that will lead to an enthusiastic and deepened commitment of their time, talents, and resources to God. (This assumes a friendly, supportive climate in the congregation which encourages persons to speak freely, accepts differences of opinion, and works toward consensus).
- to express their faith in their daily lives through their ministry to the community (for example, to teenagers and older people), and through their ministry to the world.
- to improve their skills in functioning as Christian marriage partners, parents, teachers, discussion group leaders, choir members, committee or board members, visitors, worship leaders, students of the Bible, and in other roles as Christians.

In this church the following settings with education as a prime focus contribute to accomplishing these purposes: church school, confirmation, fellowship events for adults, leadership events, and special intergenerational events. In addition, settings whose prime focus is other than education also contribute to accomplishing the educational purposes: board and committee meetings, services of worship, youth and adult choirs, camping and conferences, youth fellowship, women's fellowship and circles, and special Lenten services (such as drama, discussions).

The board of Christian education and the ministerial team are responsible for overseeing the development and integrated quality of this program. The groundwork of the parish program was laid by forming a parish education committee, with task forces that looked into possible educational settings, and then drew up the statement of educational purposes. The ministers are involved in all programs in some way.

Another church, this time in Wisconsin, reports that the covenant of the church reads:

You shall love the Lord your God with all your strength and with all your mind, and your neighbor as yourself. The congregation has accepted as ours the philosophy of the United Church Curriculum which is also based on the two great commandments. Hence our educational program is designed to help persons: (1) grow in relation with God; (2) develop trustful and responsible relationships with others; (3) become a whole person.

Church school, confirmation, and retreats are listed in this church as settings whose prime focus is educational. Even greater stress seems to be placed on using events whose prime focus is other than educational as means for accomplishing the educational purposes. Some of these events are a combination of foci. The pastor reports that the fact that all the children, grades 1-9, are visible in church every Sunday contributes substantially to the sense of wholeness in the community of faith. He says: "All pupils grades 1-9 worship with the congregation for half an hour and then report to classes for an additional hour. Twice a month we offer two simultaneous worship experiences. The one is traditional. The other is informal with education and growth as a focal point. The message is presented by a dialogue, drama, film, filmstrip, interview with a service organization, etc. This is always followed by group discussion. Grades 7-9 sometimes are included in the discussion, depending on relevance to them and their needs. We also try to give an educational thrust to our board meetings; some boards have set aside time just to grow as persons and as a board. The minister usually sets the stage for the educational thrust, but we do get good support from laity. More and more, some of our informal services are organized and led by laity, the ministers serving as monitors or resource persons. Wholeness in our educational programming is attained by the minister's watchful eye; continual evaluation of every program and project is done by the boards; and suggestions are frequently offered by concerned church members who raise questions, offer ideas, and support the concept. In order of responsibility, these persons are responsible for the development of an integrated educational program which will accomplish our educational goals; minister, fellowship committee (which plans monthly intergenerational events), the board of Christian education, and the deacons."

Clearly, in this church, education aims to help persons grow as

34

Christians. Therefore all parts of the church life, and those persons responsible for the parts, work together to develop educational settings and learning experiences that will contribute to accomplishing the educational purposes.

The church in Wisconsin which shares its life with another congregation (see page 30) developed two basic educational thrusts: (1) educational experience across age lines (including peer experiences and a learning center approach); and (2) a concentration on adult education. After a careful study, the Long Range Education Committee for the combined educational program made these recommendations to be achieved in Christian education:

1. A continued variety of approaches to education—in curriculum, methodology, and resources—to meet a greater scope of personal needs and to provide enrichment in many ways. A variety of methods introduces people to each other at different levels.
2. A joint worship experience as part of one or more Sunday's program in the longer time segments is important.
3. Brunches and shared meals should be included to serve as important fellowship features of our education program.
4. Longer time segments will allow for a variety of methods—peer groups, learning centers, family projects—within a single theme. We aren't limited to one particular method at a time.
5. We would like to see repeat performances of several successful techniques previously used: role-playing, puppetry, Shalom nursery, learning centers, Sunday music festival, family resource books, joint family potlucks, field trips (mixed ages or departmental), theater groups.
6. Each planning group is responsible for making an evaluation and submitting a written summary for the files.
7. Evaluation summaries are to be read by future groups to help them in their planning.
8. Publicity and feedback (congregational and committee) need to be expanded and refined as a vital part of the program (e.g., an information booth, telephone tape, tape messages, newsletter).
9. Some non-Sunday morning experiences should be included for all ages, possibly a home "church education" experience three or four times a year.

10. A summer experience—possibly two weeks of morning programs—could be planned to give extra depth to our school year program.

11. Key resource people in the congregations would help equip parents to teach their own children.

While the above recommendations combine both methodologies and suggestions for educational events, reference to the church's "Statement of Purpose" on page 30 will show that the educational recommendations help to accomplish that purpose by developing a community grounded in Christian faith, and relating persons to the faith and to one another in a variety of ways which meet their needs and life-styles.

DISCOVERING POSSIBILITIES FOR EDUCATION IN THE CONGREGATION'S LIFE

We have already mentioned two kinds of possibilities for learning/teaching in the life of the congregation:

1. Planned events or sequences whose *primary* focus and purpose are educational;

2. Other events, relationships, and activities in the congregation whose primary focus or purpose is some other aspect of the church's life: e.g., worship services, committee meetings, seasonal celebrations, human relationships, and so on. But in these parts of the congregational life, learning—and often unintentional teaching—do occur.

Both kinds of learning possibilities need to be taken into account in developing Christian education from a wholistic point of view. But how can churches discover what all these possibilities are?

One way is to make a two-column list and fill in each side by recall or brainstorming. For example:

Planned Events	Other Possibilities
Church School	All-Church Retreats
Youth Fellowships	Church Council Meetings
Adult Bible Study	Fellowship Hours

A second, and more fruitful, method is one that several churches have used. In a year's experimental program in the Rocky Mountain area, a dozen churches set as their goal for a year to develop education from a wholistic perspective. The first major concern was: "What are the possibilities in our church?"

37

To help answer that question, each congregation listed and analyzed a month's worth of all activities that went on in the congregation's life. The following questions were asked about each activity listed:

1. What was the event or activity?
2. How often did it occur—weekly, monthly, or how often?
3. What was the stated purpose of the event?
4. Who was in charge of the event?
5. Who (and how many) participated in the event?
6. Was the stated purpose in any way, or any degree, educational?
7. In events declared to be educational, what was accomplished educationally?
8. In events that had other purposes, was there any educational impact or by-product? If so, what was the nature of the by-product?

Each church drew up a large wall-chart to record its findings and discoveries. A mini-version of its framework is on page 39.

Any number of activities were discovered as containing one or the other kinds of learning. Here is a list of by-product or unintentional educational activities which one church discovered in addition to their regular planned program of church school, adult education, and youth fellowship. From its work in filling out the chart, this church noted the learning or teaching that might be found in each of its "by-product" discoveries:

1. *Coffee hour*: service, fellowship, communication
2. *Making church budget*: interpretation of program, values, and priorities
3. *Commissions and Boards*: need to study as Christians the relations of their work to the purpose of the church
4. *Recreation*: interpersonal relations
5. *Rendering personal service to church life and personnel*: chance to share faith and questions about it
6. *Church staff occasionally trade jobs*: to get the feel of the "other's moccasins"; stronger sense of teamwork
7. *Interpersonal relationships among members*: ushers speaking to people; atmosphere of real community
8. *Intercessory prayer*: faith in God, and knowing needs of others
9. *Expression of names of the ill and concern for them in church service*: community and sense of caring

A Wholistic Perspective on Education in a Church

1. Event	2. Frequence	3. Stated purpose	4. Was purpose educational?	5. Who was in charge?	6. Who participated?	7. What were educational accomplishments	8. Were there educational by-products? What?

10. *Helping all ages know each other*: learning to take persons seriously; community
11. *Securing of equipment*: equipment appropriate in size, usable, aids to teaching
12. *Building and conditions of rooms*: affect learning and teaching; give evidence of spirit of church
13. *Condition of equipment*: does church care about people who have to use it?
14. *Handling conflict and solving problems*: real chance for teaching and learning; shows spirit of congregation
15. *Role of decision-makers and who they are*: do they take others in on the process, or are they prima donnas? Evidence of trust/no trust, to what degree people care about the church, or how much it is a community that shares decisions
16. *Accepting people as they are*: means really learning to be and act as a Christian. As Jesus did.

Other congregations would add other educational possibilities: retreats, seasonal events, special study groups, action in the community, special projects for the world's needs, and many others. But each congregation needs to find out what it is doing that is primarily educational, and then what the other by-product learning possibilities are that must be taken into account in wholistic planning for education.

Taking all possibilities into account does not mean trying to be imperialistic about education, i.e., saying that "everything is primarily education." But being aware of these possibilities does mean these things:

1. New opportunities for planned education may present themselves. (For example, one consistory decided that it would have fifteen minutes at the beginning of every session for study of the meaning of various phases of its work.)
2. People developing the planned educational program are alert to the other learnings that may be going on elsewhere and can keep them in mind as they make their plans. Affirmative by-product learnings need to be utilized whenever possible, and sometimes it is necessary to find ways to offset negative by-product learnings.
3. Unplanned learnings combined with planned educational opportunities provide a whole or complete Christian education experience for the whole person. The examples given on pages 11-14 of several persons' experiences il-

lustrate this essential interaction of planned and unplanned, integrated by the work of the Holy Spirit through human efforts to provide the best possible opportunities for education in the faith.

2. IDENTIFY WHAT WE BELIEVE ABOUT THEOLOGY

"Theology" is sometimes a rather awesome word. To many people it suggests doctrines or creeds that must be accepted as what one believes in the Christian faith. To others it may call to mind seminary courses of study and specialized training for ministers.

Actually, theology is something in which everyone engages, whether or not he or she is aware of it. It is a process, the process of putting into words the intellectual content of faith: that is, what we understand our Christian faith to mean. Without words we cannot fully communicate or share our faith. Deeds communicate faith, of course, but words are essential too. We need to be able to talk about our ideas, or express our questions and convictions with other people, as we search for a fuller understanding of faith and seek to share the faith with others.

If we had only feelings but no intellectual content or understanding we could never think about faith, ask questions, respond to others, or participate fully in sharing the faith. The basic source of our faith—the Bible and Christian writings through the ages— would not exist unless the great experiences between God and human beings had been expressed as ideas in the spoken and written word.

"Thinking theologically" and "doing theology" are two current phrases that emphasize theology as a process in which everyone engages, rather than viewing theology as once-and-for-all statements that constitute Christian faith. Creeds and doctrines and statements of faith are expressions of theology, but they were all preceded by the process of "thinking theologically" or "doing theology."

For the Christian, theology is rooted in God as made known to us in Jesus Christ. At one level theology has a special faith language for the Christian. Familiar phrases and words with special meanings belong to the great Christian tradition: God, Jesus Christ, the Holy Spirit, the Bible as the Word of God, the church as the Body of Christ, mission, sin, forgiveness, salvation, reconciliation, and other such words. For many people the rich meaning in

41

these words of experience and faith is clear; for others it is not clear, and interpretations vary from generation to generation according to situations and experiences of the times. But all these words bear deep significance in their relation to God and God's purposes and revelation in Jesus Christ. They need to be reclaimed for each generation and translated into contemporary experience and words. Even when these words are not used specifically, the Christian bases thinking theologically on the Bible, the historic faith and life of the church, and his or her own life experience.

Theological thinking is thus not limited to use of this special Christian faith language. Theology deals with the ultimate—the most important purposes and values of life. Every time we think about a serious matter, or raise an important question and relate it to that which we value most, we are thinking theologically. Terminology may be everyday language, but theology will be implied. The process of theological or faith inquiry is present. As Christians, we are dealing with what is ultimate for us: faith and our commitment to God and Jesus Christ. For example, here is a comment: "If God really cares about everyone, why is there so much violence going on today?" The implied theology in this comment questions God's way of working. It also deals with the question of human beings' responsibility for their own actions, as well as the question of evil and its source.

Many people who might make no claim to thinking theologically are often surprised to discover that some of their questions are really unconsciously rooted in the fundamentals of the faith as mentioned above and discussed more fully in sections of Chapter 3. Discovering this rootage helps people take a thoughtful look at their ultimate or most important values and consider whether those values are basically Christian.

A few sample comments with theological implications follow, along with statements of implied theology that some persons have made. Questions such as these could be used in helping people to enter into the process of thinking theologically.

Question or Comment	*Implied Theology*
Why should I work so hard when others get by with doing less and get paid as much as I do? Doesn't God care?	(Is God just? Do people get by with no punishment? Is this kind of thing sinful?)

43

Some religious people say they're saved but I am not. How do they know? And what *is* being saved?

(What is the meaning of salvation? When does it occur—now, or in the future? Is it important to us?)

People who are really crooked seem to get ahead in business further than some more honest people. Why? How can God be just and let that be?

(Is God really at work in this world? Does God care? Does God really affect our lives?)

Why should there be so many hungry people in the world today, with all our technology? What does God expect us in America to do about it all?

(Is there really a God who cares? What is our human responsibility for using our abilities? What's the connection between us and other people?)

Doesn't liberation really mean letting each person do his or her own thing? Isn't that freedom under God?

(Does anyone really care what goes on? Do we have any obligation to be concerned for others? What does God give us the right to do?

Does praying really do any good? What am I supposed to pray for, and how do I know how God answers?

(What is prayer? How do I relate to God? Does God know that individuals exist—or—care?)

Theology is really unavoidable for the Christian. To refuse to call one's beliefs theology may be trying to avoid sharing honestly with others. Part of the job of Christian education is to encourage people to be willing consciously to think theologically, and to share their thinking with others. At the same time our educational ministries should give people help in discovering how to test the adequacy of their theology in the light of the Bible and Christian tradition. There is always room for growth in theology, as there is in faith. People must be willing to face each day with the commitments and beliefs they have, hoping for more light and understanding as they work at living and thinking theologically.

A CONGREGATION'S THEOLOGICAL APPROACH
Just as persons have their individual theological approach and point of view, so church congregations tend to have a basic theological stance or emphasis. This does not mean that all

members think alike about the faith, or that everyone conforms in word and deed. Diversity is to be treasured in a congregation. But in a general or basic sort of way, most congregations tend to have an approach to the faith compatible with the ways in which the congregation and its members express and live out their commitments.

In designing educational ministries from the wholistic approach, it is important to know what the congregation's general theological stance is. It is equally important to discover the spread of theological differences held by various members. Knowing what the basic core of the theological approach is, together with the range of diversity, will help to make possible harmony-within-diversity in what is taught, preached, and used as the basis of mission and decisions affecting the life of the congregation.

For example, if a congregation's basic theology requires that all people subscribe to the doctrine that certain personal life practices are required of those who believe in Jesus Christ, that congregation's educational program may focus on cultivating those practices and bringing other people to accept this doctrine. But if another congregation holds that God calls them to express the Christian gospel by serving the needs of a varied and changing neighborhood, its educational ministry will probably be designed to make a study of Jesus' life and his ministry central in order to carry out in as many ways as possible his commands to those who would follow him, and so serve the needs of the community.

To find out the congregation's theological approach is, therefore, essential for designing a wholistic educational ministry. What is dealt with in the educational program needs to be in harmony with the general stance of the congregation.

SOME SAMPLE THEOLOGICAL STATEMENTS

Many churches have statements of purpose or belief that express theological points of view. Here are examples from several local churches in various parts of the country.

1. The avowed purpose of this church shall be to worship God, to preach and teach the gospel of Jesus Christ, to celebrate the Sacraments, to realize Christian fellowship and unity within this church, the community and the Church Universal, to render loving service to all mankind and to strive for righteousness, justice and peace. (*From a church in a small midwestern community.*)

2. The objectives of our program of Christian education are to direct the pupil toward discovering who he or she is in relation to God and to fellow human beings, with emphasis in experiencing relationships and feelings with God and persons, rather than just being told about them. The program will be biblically oriented so as to reveal to us how God acts in the world today. We will seek the formation of mature Christians who will exhibit the following characteristics:

- an ability to live without need of absolute certainty;
- a conscience so developed as to be able to take individual responsibility for one's own actions;
- a continuing awareness of an individual's worth and the worth of others;
- a continuing search for new ways to use this awareness and to encourage its use by the community for the betterment of the community;
- a respectful attitude that listens to others for the purpose of understanding;
- a faith flexible enough to be able to integrate all knowledge;
- a faith which is creative and allows one to carry on a constant dialogue with one's surroundings and leads to a renewal of life.

(From a young church in a medium-sized college city.)

The above began as a statement of purpose of Christian education, but is also fundamentally a theological basis for the life of the particular congregation which developed it.

3. Our approach stems from worship as the journey of the people holding their life-journey up to God for transformation. Essential elements are:

- GOD: ground of our being, energizer (one who empowers), focus on the Christ event, our accountability to God;
- PEOPLE: we celebrate our being in contemplation of the journey of our life, our deeds and misdeeds, our potential, our response to God who has acted and is acting, our solidarity as a people given grace by God;
- THE JOURNEY OF THE PEOPLE: in each worship experience celebrating life's journey of birth, separation, wandering, returning and repentance, death by putting off the old ways, resurrection in putting on the new life

with expectancy and hope. In community we learn, grow, and act, supported by the community that not only sends us but supports and sustains us. *(From a community-minded church in a large town.)*

4. The purposes of this church are to promote the worship of God and teachings of our Lord Jesus Christ. This church is a free Protestant Christian church. We, its members, are bound together by a simple covenant in which we express our common loyalty to the Lord Jesus Christ and our mutual purpose to follow him in a life of love to God and to our fellow men. We accept the Holy Scriptures as our guide to faith and service. Believing in a broad and comprehensive basis of membership which permits wide latitude of individual differences of belief, opinion and interpretation, we welcome to our fellowship all who share our faith and purposes. The covenant of this church is: Believing in Jesus Christ as our Redeemer and Lord, trusting in His revelation of the loving Heavenly Father, acknowledging our dependence upon the Holy Spirit, we covenant with each other to worship and work together as loyal disciples of Jesus, to live a life of righteousness and brotherly love, and to do all within our power to promote the reign of God's will in all human relations. *(From large suburban church in a metropolitan area.)*

These four quotations of samples of theological approaches of individual congregations differ in style of expression, points of emphasis, scope, and particular ways of expressing the gospel and faith. Yet each is a theological statement. Designing a Christian education program from the wholistic approach for each congregation would probably result in different kinds of settings, different styles of leadership, different uses of resources, considerable variety in worship and celebration, and wide diversity in educational format and events. Education in each church should reflect the emphases of the theological approach.

EXPLORING AND DETERMINING THE THEOLOGICAL APPROACH

What if your congregation does not have such a formal statement of theology? What are some ways of exploring and determining the theological approach? And even if the congregation does have a statement, perhaps it needs to be checked to make sure that it reflects faith and its expression in today's world and is one that should be taken into account in designing an educational program.

Here are some suggestions for carrying out this exploration. Doing this study, incidentally, will be an excellent process. It may be carried out by the educational board, or by a committee assigned by the congregation. It should prove a refresher and stimulant for all persons involved; findings should be shared in some way with the entire congregation.

STUDY A STATEMENT OF FAITH OR CREED USED BY THE CONGREGATION. Any of the classic creeds of the Christian church might be used, such as the Apostles' Creed or the Nicene Creed, provided they are at some time or another used in congregational worship. Another possibility is the United Church of Christ Statement of Faith.

The committee may prepare a list of questions: Do you agree/disagree with this statement? Does it have meaning for you personally? Which of the parts seem most significant to you? Which need clarification in meaning for today's life? What words need fresh interpretation?

Questions could be circulated, with the theological statement, to various church groups such as the church council or consistory, diaconates, elders, trustees, youth groups, women's and men's or mixed study groups. Each group could be asked to consider the list of questions and respond. In the light of their discussions and responses, groups might also be asked to develop their own theological statements. From these results the educational board or committee could determine what theological agreements and diversities exist, and could formulate a set of theological foundations for the educational program.

FIND OUT WHAT THE PEOPLE KNOW ABOUT THE BIBLE AS A WHOLE. Teaching the Bible is a universal demand of Christian education in most churches. Yet, educational committees have discovered, people may mean many different things when they say, "I want the Bible to be taught." People responsible for educational ministries should find out just what is meant and wanted.

One exercise might be to prepare a list of questions to be asked of youth groups, church governing bodies, other special church groups. These questions could aim to find out what members think the Bible is. For example:

48

Check the descriptions of the Bible which most nearly fit your idea of what the Bible is and complete a statement of what the description means:

_____ The Bible is the Word of God. To me this means _____

_____

_____ The Bible is the history of God's people. To me this means

_____

_____ The Bible is a sourcebook of inspirational passages. To me this means _____

_____

_____ The Bible is a channel through which God speaks to us today. To me this means _____

_____

_____ The Bible is a rule book for right and wrong. To me this means _____

_____

You may, of course, prefer to make up your own list of statements describing what the Bible is. But be sure to allow space for respondents to explain what their answers mean to them, because explanations (or lack of them) will tell you much more than just checks in front of a description. A book that may prove helpful to committees in devising a list of questions is *Exploring the Bible with Children* by Dorothy Jean Furnish (Abingdon, 1975), especially sections I and III. (Section IV will give the educational committee some good ideas of settings for teaching the Bible when time for program development comes.)

A second exercise that might also be used with church groups would be to ask each group to list the passages from the Bible with which they believe every youth/adult ought to be familiar, and to identify what the passages disclose about God and humankind and their relationships. Such a listing would reveal to the education committee whether respondents are familiar with the Bible as a whole, what meanings stand out for them, and what they think the Bible is. One group that did this exercise discovered that the passages they thought most important were all from the Old Testament. This discovery caused the group to rethink what its idea of "Teaching the Bible" was.

Answers to either of the above exercises will have theological content or implications. From them the education committee can get basic ideas of what members think or believe theologically, and can use this information in their educational planning.

DO A HYMN STUDY. The great hymns of the church are all theological statements; so also are many of the newer songs coming from folk interpretation, along with certain gospel hymns and well-loved spirituals.

The Christian education committee might ask members of the congregation to name their three favorite hymns. Again, ask for a brief statement saying why this hymn is a favorite and what the person considers its relation to the faith to be. One person who was asked this question listed "He Who Would Valiant Be" because it expressed the Christian's call to be a pilgrim serving God; "A Mighty Fortress Is Our God" because it exuded power and strength and security that comes from trusting God; "Blest Be the Tie That Binds" because it expressed the love and closeness of companionship in the community of faith. These selections and comments told the Christian education committee that for this member God was very real, and the ground of life, and that the fellowship of the community of faith was important.

Another approach to hymn study would be for the Christian education committee to work with the pastor and worship committee—or those responsible with the pastor for the Sunday services of worship—to select a "Hymn of the Month," to be used in each service with explanations of the meaning of a stanza each Sunday. The hymn may be sung; used as a reponsive reading; serve as a musical "dialogue" between choir and congregation for alternate singing of stanzas, and the like. The Hymn of the Month may be chosen in relation to the services, but from a list of favorites that the congregation may be asked to nominate. This practice can be both educational for the congregation and informative to the Christian education committee about the theological thinking of the congregation.

Explanatory notes on the meaning of hymns may also be included on church bulletins or in church newspapers. Even the most "literate" church members often fail to think about the theological ideas they are singing. Surprising reactions often occur when the process of thinking theologically about hymns is activated.

STUDY BOOKS OR SHORT BOOKLETS ON THEOLOGY. The Christian education committee may benefit from reading and reacting to books or short publications on Christian beliefs. This could be an especially appropriate activity after some of the ways of sampling congregational theological thinking have been tried. Committee members may read and analyze the books as points of view with which to compare and discuss what the members of the congregation have disclosed. The pastor could very well be the consultant for this activity. He or she may suggest items to read, and be a consultant to the committee in its discussions. The temptation to let the pastor do all the reading or sharing out of his or her own study should be resisted! Committee members need to undergo the work of reading and thinking theologically themselves. Then the pastor can be adviser and helper by asking questions, suggesting points that committee members may overlook when comparing their own thoughts with the congregation's ideas, and the like. As an enabler, the pastor will be rendering an important educational service!

Here are a few suggestions for reading that have been found useful in many churches. Your pastor will have others to suggest. Magazines such as RISK and other ecumenical publications may also prove useful. Many of these may be found in church libraries or your pastor's library.

    a. Shinn, Roger and Williams, Daniel, *We Believe*, United Church Press.

    b. Williams, Daniel Day, *What Present Day Theologians Are Thinking*, rev. ed. (See libraries as a source of this book.)

    c. Brown, Robert McAfee, *Is Faith Obsolete?*, Westminster.

    d. Cone, James, H., *A Black Theology of Liberation,* Lippincott.

    e. Russell, Letty, *Human Liberation in a Feminist Perspective,* Westminster.

STUDY THE THEOLOGICAL ASSUMPTIONS OF CHRISTIAN EDUCATION: SHARED APPROACHES. Several Protestant denominations in the cooperative group known as JED (Joint Educational Development) have developed four total approaches to church education which aim to help congregations see their educational ministry in relation to the whole church. Resource materials are a component of each of the four approaches, so also are theological and educational foundations. Your church's Christian education committee might profitably take some statements of these theological bases and use them for study by the committee and as an instrument for securing congregational reaction (agree or disagree). Here are statements of the CE:SA "Theological

Affirmations" as taken from the booklet *Christian Education: Shared Approaches–An Overview* by Robert E. Koenig.* The title of each approach precedes each group of affirmations, but the affirmations may be used independently of the titles for this special purpose of identifying your church's beliefs about theology.

Knowing the Word

1. Scripture is an authoritative witness for the church. The Holy Spirit inspired the authors and illumines the readers.
2. The Old Testament will be interpreted historically, but applied in the light of the New Testament, which fulfills the Old.
3. The Bible records God's revelation in Christ. It confronts persons with the promises and demands of the gospel for all of life, both personal and social.

Interpreting the Word

1. The Bible, a book for the people of God, is normative for the Christian community. Each individual Christian is responsible, within the context of the Christian community, for interpreting the Bible so that it might inform contemporary reflection and action.
2. The message of the Bible, though culturally conditioned, transcends all times and places. No interpretation can be considered as final, but the experience of other times and other cultures can help people today to gain insight into the biblical message.
3. A faithful reading and study of the Bible may result in a transforming encounter with God through the Holy Spirit, who inspired the writing of the Scriptures.

Living the Word

1. God, the Creator and Sustainer of all, works among people and nations for their salvation through Jesus Christ. The approach [Living the Word] draws from the biblical record, the experience of the church throughout history, and present-day perceptions of God's working. It probes the relationships among persons and with God in Christ to help persons discover who they are and what their human relationships mean.
2. Theology is faith in search of understanding, process rather than product, active inquiry, the responsibility of the whole church.

---

*Copyright © 1975 by United Church Press. Used by permission.

3. The Bible as the record of God's revelation confronts persons with the concerns of the gospel in relation to faith, values, relationships, social responsibility, hope and discipleship.
4. The church is the people of God in Jesus Christ, sustained by the Holy Spirit, who sends it forth in mission, guiding and empowering its witness and worship.

Doing the Word
1. The good news of salvation speaks of God at work in the world and applies to societal as well as individual needs, with special attention to the oppressed and the powerless.
2. The people of God are called to discern how God is working in restoring humanity, restructuring society, and caring for all creation.
3. The church as a corporate body is called to witness by word and deed to the gospel as it relates to the pressing issues confronting society.

Reading these theological affirmations may remind you of the paragraphs on page 41 of this section about the special Christian faith language. A number of those special words are used in these CE:SA theological affirmations. The Christian education committee might profitably relate its examination of these affirmations to that special language, and then to everyday-language ways of expressing theological thinking and ideas. In relating these affirmations to the faith language, list statements that relate to as many of the terms on page 41 as possible. Included certainly will be statements about God, Jesus Christ, the Bible, salvation, mission, and many others.

If you use these affirmations as test statements with other groups, try such church official bodies as consistory, church council, deacons, elders, trustees. Ask not only whether they agree or disagree, but also for indication of statements that need additional explanation to make them clear in everyday language, or for words whose meaning needs additional amplification. From such responses may come grist for possible sermons by the pastor, or special adult study groups, as well as identification of what your church members' theological point of view is.

MAKING YOUR OWN STATEMENT
After the Christian education committee has worked with the congregation, and within its own ranks, to identify your church's general point of view and beliefs about theology, a concluding step

53

will be to write some kind of summary statement of what seems to have been discovered. Refer to the four sample church theological statements on pages 44-47 of this section. Yours may take a variety of forms: a complete statement; an open-ended statement to be continued; or perhaps a list of beliefs that seem most clearly to express your congregation's general stance in theology. Whatever the form, such a summary is an essential component of the process of designing your educational program from a wholistic point of view.

3. IDENTIFY WHAT WE BELIEVE ABOUT EDUCATION
UNINTENTIONAL OR UNPLANNED LEARNING

Learning is a continuous process, an integral part of all of life. Whether we realize it or not, we are constantly responding to stimuli, physically, mentally, and emotionally, and these responses become part of our beings. Information and sensations are taken in by all our senses. A major portion of these learnings are unplanned or are by-products of activities with primary purposes that are labelled differently from what the unplanned responses may be. In educational programs some stimuli are carefully planned, but these planned programs provide only a small portion of the sources from which we learn.

Much of the unplanned kind of learning—some would say *real* learning—comes from observation, imitation and experimentation. Leaders in a church nursery group were sympathetically amused by a little girl using the toy telephone in the housekeeping corner. She stood with shoulders thrust slightly back, legs apart, chin up, one hand on her hip and spoke in a strident voice, demanding to know: "*When* is that plumber coming?" Quite unconsciously this child had learned the body language and tone of indignation and exasperation that applied to a frustrating situation. An incident at home had no doubt had a powerful effect!

Another example of observation, combined with bits of "planned" learning, is the story of a seven-year-old boy who was looking about his home after church one Sunday. After a while he asked his father, "Is it true that the church is God's house?" "Of course," responded his father. "God sure doesn't take as good care of his house as we do ours!" replied the boy. The father happened to be chairperson of the board of trustees of the church.

At its very next meeting the board surveyed the church building and voted to make needed repairs and to repaint the rather dilapidated parish house and church school rooms.

In the wholistic approach to Christian education we must be acutely aware of the continuous, unplanned learning that influences the actions and reactions of all the people in our churches—for good or ill. In reclaiming Christian education, we must keep these learnings in mind and take them into account as we work on planned educational opportunities designed to enable persons to grow in their understanding of the faith and their commitment to Christ and his church.

When we teach students that the church is the household of God, we want to be sure that all the experiences the students are having in the church reflect this teaching and make its meaning clear. If some people are not welcome in the church for one reason or another, or if young people are excluded from the decision-making processes of the church, the students are getting two different sets of information about the church—the verbal, and the experiential that contradicts the verbal. If the negative learnings cannot be changed immediately, the students should be encouraged to discuss the problems openly with church leaders, both to communicate their learnings and to work toward overcoming the problems.

We must also build on the unplanned learnings. The incident of the boy who was concerned because God's house was not as well cared for as his own opened up opportunities to talk about what is meant when we call the church "God's house," to discuss the responsibility of all church members to share in taking care of the church building, and to study the particular responsibilities of the trustees or other group for the physical upkeep of the building.

Planned learning can no more be separated from unplanned learning than the church can be separated from all that goes on outside the church. The experiences people have outside the church, their personal problems and the problems of the world, cannot be checked at the church door. The wholistic approach to education recognizes the interrelation of all learning, and considers this when developing planned education programs.

INTENTIONAL OR PLANNED LEARNING

There are many descriptive definitions of what goes on in education (intentional or planned learning): to learn reading, writing and arithmetic; to learn to think; to learn to appreciate art, music and literature; to learn good citizenship; to prepare oneself for earning a living. Each definition is accurate as far as it goes, but education is all of these and more.

The word *educate* comes from the Latin *educere*, which means "to lead forth." This implies process, action, direction, exploration of a varied and enriching environment. We might picture education as a process of opening doors; inviting persons to walk through them; and guiding persons as they explore the new environment of ideas and information, new skills, new appreciations, new values and feelings, and act upon the new opportunities that lie beyond the doors.

MAKING EDUCATION CHRISTIAN

Sometimes people become concerned because in the school of the church we use many of the same methods, and even similar subject matter, as that found in general education. In Christian education we *do* open many of the same doors as in general education, but we open them from different angles, and emphasize different aspects of the new environment beyond the doors. When we use learning activities that help young children develop their new skills of reading and writing, for example, we open the door from an angle that enables children to learn that their abilities are gifts from God. We also help them to realize that they are persons of worth, children of God, able to do many things. Or, when we open the door of learning good citizenship, we open it from an angle that helps persons learn Christian values, and how to make moral and ethical decisions that involve them in working for justice, freedom and liberation for oppressed people. Whatever doors we open, whether in the school of the church or in other kinds of learning opportunities in the life of the congregation, our purpose is to work toward fulfilling the church's mission.

One of the problems with Christian education has been our tendency to think of education, not as opening doors to new experiences and new understandings of our faith and mission, but as a forced-feeding process. In our anxiety to have children and youth, especially, hear the faith story, we have imposed upon them our adult understandings of that story before they have really heard the story for itself and are ready or able to grasp its deeper meanings. We have been like the sower who cast his seeds on rocky ground. The plants sprang up, but they soon withered because there was no depth to the soil. Time and effort are required for soil to become enriched. We have to prepare the soil with experiences of love, forgiveness, sharing, giving, and celebration so that the seeds sown will grow and bring forth much fruit.

Some parents—and some churches—err the opposite way. They neither open doors nor force-feed. They believe that when persons (even young children) are "ready" they will open the doors for themselves or ask that they be opened. This is rather like playing tag blindfolded: there is a lot of aimless running around, and an occasional accidental tag. In this approach, persons may have a number of learning experiences in the church but no effort is made to help these persons coordinate these learnings or to stimulate them to ask for guidance and opportunities to learn more about the faith.

How do the people in your church see Christian education? Do they see it as opening doors to a rich environment with many learning possibilities—and with the risk that students may follow paths of understanding or commitment other than those we might choose for them? Or do they think of planned Christian education as an opportunity to "hand on" (force-feed) the faith to others? Or do they think planned education should not be offered until persons ask for it?

HOW PERSONS LEARN
The persons responsible for planned educational ministries in your church will be helped to wise decisions if they are aware of how persons learn, particularly how they learn in relation to their total growth and development as persons.

The learning process is one of exploration, discovery, making sense of the discovery (comprehension, conceptualization), and acting upon this comprehension. Or, to put it another way, learning is that part of the educational process that affects the minds, emotions, and will power of participants as they go through the open doors, explore the new environment, absorb and integrate new ideas, experiences and information into their lives, act upon these, and move toward more opening doors and new opportunities.

Learners do not progress through these doors at the same rate, or move in the same directions once they venture through them. *What* they learn and *how* depends in large part on what persons bring with them: personal background; interest and concern with

the area of study; appropriate skills and experiences; ability to comprehend. Over the years many studies have been made about ways people learn, and why.

According to one set of studies, persons learn by being given small bits of information or other "content" or "input." They are immediately asked to use this input, usually to answer a question or perform a certain action (feedback). Their responses are checked at once against the initial input (reinforcement or correction). If responses are correct, the persons are given new bits of input and the process continues. If a response is incorrect, the person involved repeats the step as many times as necessary to get the correct response before moving on. This approach to learning is the basis of programmed instruction. It is a useful way to learn certain kinds of information and to develop certain skills. In the church this might be used effectively for developing basic skills in finding one's way around in the Bible, learning the chronology of the biblical story, or the sequence of events in church history, and the like.

The wholistic approach to education, however, is concerned with the development of whole persons, not just with a cognitive learning here, a behavioral modification there, or development of a particular skill. Concern with the whole person is deeply imbedded in Christian tradition. We read in the Gospel according to Luke that: "Jesus increased in wisdom [mental growth], in stature [physical growth], and in favor with God [spiritual growth] and man [emotional and social development]" (Luke 2:52).

Another concept of the learning process, the developmental theory, is wholistic in its approach. Through all kinds of testing and observation over many years, educators, psychologists and other scientists have discovered the characteristic physical, mental and emotional abilities and needs of persons at each stage of their development. These findings and their implications for how people learn are important for parents, teachers, ministers and other members of our congregations to know as they plan and carry out effective educational ministries in the church. Following is a brief review of some of the important developmental abilities and needs that should be taken into consideration in planning for church education.

INFANTS AND TODDLERS (BIRTH THROUGH TWO YEARS). The first two or three years of life are filled with basic learnings crucial to future development. Even the experience of birth itself may have a crucial impact on the total development of a person. Recent studies testify that babies born in a quiet room with dim lights, followed by a few minutes of rest on the mother's stomach before the umbilical cord is cut, have developed more quickly and with more abilities than comparable children whose delivery was more standard or traumatic.

In the first years of life children are busy discovering themselves as physical beings able to sit up, crawl, walk, begin to feed themselves and to talk. By the time of their first birthday, most children have developed memory: that is, they can identify persons and objects they have seen frequently. These very young children need lots of love, encouragement, care, and approval of each developing ability to help them feel good about themselves.

These early years are times of development of large muscles of the arms and legs, which means that children need space and equipment for walking, running, climbing, lifting, pushing, pulling. As children grow in their ability to walk, their world expands and they have more freedom to explore. This means that both parents and teachers have to put limits on children's freedom without squelching their curiosity and growing self-assertiveness. The children's growing vocabularies reflect their experiences as they learn words associated with people, objects, and rules: Mama, Daddy, kitty, chair, mustn't touch, drink your milk.

The very young are curious about other small children, but as objects rather than as friends or playmates. They will play alongside other children, but usually not *with* them in cooperative play such as building a stack of blocks.

By age two, most children are developing the ability to stand apart from parents, but they may become panicky when these adults upon whom they depend are out of sight for a long time— and a few minutes may be a "long time" for some children. Some two-year-olds brought to the church explore this strange place and discover friendly grown-ups who love and care for them. They learn that there is a special place for them with "just right" toys and books. After a few sessions these children begin to associate the love and enjoyment they experience with *church*: "My church." They also begin to associate, at a preconceptual level, their experiences of love, understanding, and care with the ideas of God and Jesus.

Unfortunately, other young children learn just the opposite. If

they have not previously had successful experiences of being separated from their parents for short periods of time, they may be frightened by being brought and left in a strange place with strange grownups (no matter how friendly and loving they are), strange children, and strange toys. Steps can be taken to prevent this from happening. Both parents and children can learn about the love of God as it is expressed in the acts of nursery leaders if the leaders make the time and effort to visit children in their homes and invite them to come to church at a time when no other children are there. Thus the child, secure in the presence of a parent or other well-known adult, can get acquainted with the new place and its equipment, and better acquainted with the nursery leader. The experience of coming to the toddlers' *group* will then be less traumatic.

Too often we underestimate the importance of church care for the very young: "They are too little to understand." So we have teenagers or a succession of adults who, with the best intentions, often fail to give the children the love and security they need. These young children cannot conceptualize or verbalize their learnings, but, deep inside, feelings and attitudes are being formed about the church and about God. When these children become teenagers and adults able to make commitments to Christ and the church, these early experiences will subconsciously influence their decisions. The church that is really concerned for the wholistic approach to education, and the church of the future, will do its best to ensure that all the experiences of young children within the church community reflect the love of God made known in Jesus Christ.

An interesting report comes from a church that had made a special effort to provide good experiences for the children on the cradle roll and in the church nursery. The members of the congregation took seriously their commitments at baptism to help each child to grow in the faith. Both the minister and lay people called in the homes. The strongest leaders were assigned to work with the small children. Nearly twenty years later a check on what had happened to those children showed that every one of them was an active, committed Christian. Several had moved to other churches, but none had "dropped out."

THREES AND FOURS. Children in this age group are developing rapidly in their ability to relate to other children. They begin to play together, which brings both pleasure and conflict. Teachers and parents have to make careful judgments about whether to intervene or let the children work out their problems for themselves. The children need experience in solving conflicts, but not when their personhood is threatened beyond their ability to cope.

Three- and four-year-olds are eager for new information. They enjoy short stories, pictures, records, objects to touch and examine; but they do not distinguish much between symbols and reality. A chair seen in a certain light may appear to be a bear, and that bear is a real animal to the child. In one family the three-year-old daughter suddenly refused to go upstairs alone. When her parents asked why, the child said she was afraid of the witch. Further prodding helped the parents to discover that the "witch" was actually a picture of Jesus hung on the wall at the stair landing. When the picture was taken down and shown to the child in the living room she recognized it as a picture of Jesus. When it was replaced on the wall of the stairway, however, she again refused to go up the stairs because of the witch. The parents had to remove the picture. Such misconceptions and inability to respond to logic are common at this age level, and adult reasoning cannot change them. In a year or so this girl's perceptive abilities will develop so that she will be able to recognize the picture in her hands in the living room and the picture hung on the stair wall as the same picture. But at this younger stage, attempts by parents or teachers to force "correct" perceptions may further confuse children or cause them to doubt themselves.

By the same token, these children are unable to recognize the intentions behind their own or others' actions. When a child is hit or bitten by another child, the reaction of the first child is usually as much surprise as hurt. The child does not understand why the other child hit him or her, nor does the one who did the hitting understand the motive that made her or him strike out at the other child. An overreaction by an adult to the incident, however, will make the hitter feel guilty—not so much over what he or she has done, but the fact that it has displeased the teacher—and the child who was hit may become more dependent on adult protection. The best reaction in such a situation is to put an arm around each and say to the one child: "You must not hit other people" or "I cannot let you hit other people." To the other child the adult may say: "I am sorry Terry hit you." A hug or kiss will make this child happy again. The child who did the hitting may be given some clay to pound or a pillow to punch to work off strong feelings.

Guilt is also incurred when adults overreact to children's initiatives that lead them into catastrophes. A four-year-old wants to be helpful and tries to pour the juice, with much of it landing on the table and floor. The helpful parent or teacher thanks the child for his or her effort and helps the child clean up the mess. The adult can then say: "The pitcher was too full and heavy for you. I will pour some of it and then you can try again when there is just the right amount in the pitcher." This takes considerable self-control on the part of the adult, but it pays big dividends in the self-esteem of the child.

If children are to learn and develop as whole persons, they will make many mistakes in these active years, often with unhappy results. They need adults who will help them to correct their mistakes and develop self-control. We cannot and should not keep them from feelings of guilt and shame for activities that are not acceptable to others, but we need to help them overbalance their bad feelings about themselves with good feelings, so that they can move on successfully to the next stage.

MIDDLE CHILDHOOD (AGES 5–8). The world of the five- and six-year-old is busy and full of interest. These children do not make much distinction, if any, between play, fantasy, and reality. Play and fantasy are real, and reality is play and fantasy. Children playing space travel become, for the time, space travelers. Chairs or boxes are spaceships. The doorstep *is* a strange planet. The reality of reading is a different kind of play, of putting letters and syllables together to make a word to read or say or spell. Fairy stories are real. With so many wonders all around them, why question that a goose can lay a golden egg?

We have to remember that for children *play* is not necessarily synonymous with *fun*, although it is usually enjoyable. Play is children's *work* through which they experiment and make sense of their world. Play is the way they learn. In our Christian education planning for early and middle childhood we must try to put ourselves into the children's shoes and utilize various forms of play as our basic teaching method.

As children move into the latter part of middle childhood (ages seven and eight), they begin to shift from play to more systematic ways of learning. They can begin to think concretely and transfer learnings from one area to another. They can think in terms of big, medium, and small, whether these refer to sizes or to the relation of numbers in an arithmetic problem. What used to be play now becomes project development—building a spaceship from cartons, making model planes, collecting and pressing leaves to use in making Thanksgiving place mats. Another aspect of play begins to be channeled into organized games and sports as the children become more closely related to their peers.

At the beginning of this stage, children are essentially egocentric. They cannot put themselves into the place of other persons in order to look at a situation from different viewpoints. One of the major learning tasks of these middle childhood years is to discover, through social interaction with children from differing backgrounds, that there are other points of view that need to be considered.

Five- and six-year-olds are also literalists. They accept statements by adults as absolute. In the church we must be clear and specific. For teachers and parents concerned with moral development, it is especially important to recognize children's literalism. It is not enough to say: "You must not take things that do not belong to others without permission." The child needs to be told that the money on the table is for paying for the newspaper or that the cookies are being saved for dinner.

A parent was greatly upset to discover a large lump of clay in her first-grader's pocket after church school. She called the teacher to ask what would be the best way to handle the situation. The understanding teacher recognized that the child had not meant to steal the clay, only to borrow it to continue the enjoyment he had had with it during the class session. In the next session, the teacher talked with all the children, explaining that the supplies were there for everyone to use while in church school, but the children could not borrow the clay or the crayons or other materials to take home because they might get lost or forgotten, and then the children would not have the things they needed to work with in church school. The child's guilt for taking the clay was eased by the fact that the adult treated his error as a mistake rather than as a deliberate wrongdoing.

OLDER CHILDHOOD (AGES 8–12). By age seven or eight most children begin to be more flexible in their thinking and can sort out reality and fantasy. They may begin, for example, to realize that Santa is fantasy and Jesus was a person. (In later childhood they may question that reality, but at this level they accept adult statements of reality.) They also begin to organize and manage the information they have accumulated over the years, and they begin to pursue knowledge because of their own interests. One third-grader got very interested in names, and spent hours looking through the Bible to see how many names of his friends and family he could find. In the process he also came across many names that struck him as funny, and he began using these as nicknames for his friends. Other children in this age group become interested in starting aquariums and learning about tropical fish, or they start rock or stamp collections and the like.

In this later period of middle childhood, children tend to become perfectionists. They will write and erase, write and erase, write and erase until they are satisfied with the appearance or spelling of a word. These children may also begin to doubt their abilities and develop feelings of inferiority when they cannot do some things as well as others do. Adults need to help them by assigning tasks within their abilities, praising them when they work well, encouraging and helping them to do their best when they want to give up because they are having difficulty or are frustrated because others have accomplished the task with seeming ease.

Christian education leaders need to be alert to the abilities and limitations of each child and provide a variety of learning experiences in the church so that each child can make significant achievements and develop good feelings about himself or herself. This does not mean that we do not challenge children to work at assignments that may be difficult for them, but we combine these challenges with opportunities to use their talents fruitfully.

An example of this is the story of Peter. Peter developed somewhat slowly as a child, and his parents wisely delayed an extra year before starting him in public school. Even so, Peter had difficulty keeping up with other, younger, members of his class in reading. His reading difficulties bothered him in church school also. Then, when Peter was in fourth grade, his older brother became an acolyte. This intrigued Peter greatly and he developed an overwhelming ambition to become an acolyte. Fortunately, Peter's need to do something to bolster his self-esteem was recognized by his parents, his teachers and his minister, so when Peter entered fifth grade he was invited to try out to be an acolyte. Because of what he had learned from his older brother, Peter passed the tryout with flying colors, and became the youngest acolyte the church had ever had. The by-products of Peter's success as an acolyte were many. He learned many things about the service of worship to share with the other children in his class; more importantly, he read with less hesitation and entered readily into discussion, sure of his ability to contribute.

Most children in this age group are curious about the world around them, people and customs of other lands, different ethnic groups, about the past and the future. They can be guided to use this curiosity and interest to pursue information and then use their mental abilities to organize and conceptualize their findings. This is a good time for children to begin to delve into their Christian heritage, to begin to put together the story of the Bible, the life of Jesus, the broad outlines of church history.

At this age children also begin to ask rather deep theological questions: "Why (not how) was I born?" "Did we create God, or did God give us the belief in God?" "The Bible says that God created the universe out of nothing. How can nothing become something?" "What is the nothing that the universe was created from?" The task of parents and teachers is to encourage the children to seek answers and to continue to raise questions, *not* to impose adult answers upon the children, and run the risk in so doing of squelching the child's curiosity. An adult may say: "This is what I think, but you may find different answers now and as you grow older." Adults also have the responsibility to give informational answers and suggestions needed by the children, or to direct them to resources to search out information.

Younger children may accept adult-made rules without questioning whether or not they are just, but older children begin to question adult authority and are very much concerned with fairness in play and in interpersonal relationships. They recognize ways in which their values and the values of their families differ from values held by other members of their peer group and their families. When values come into conflict, these children have some ability to deal with the differences, especially if an understanding adult helps them to look at the issues from all sides.

One of the major phenomena of this older childhood age group is the development of gangs or tight circles of friends. These children need to belong. They want to belong to a close-knit peer group, to a family unit, to the church, to their community and country. The church can maximize this need for belonging by initiating children more fully into the life and mission of the church. The children can join the junior choir, help occasionally

with the ushering or in the coffee hour, share some of their projects in the service of worship, and participate actively in intergenerational programs or retreats. In churches where formal membership is closely related to confirmation, older children may feel left out because they are not considered full members. Some terminology needs to be developed to emphasize belonging. Children might be called junior members or apprentice members, or we might reclaim the term *catechumen,* "one receiving instruction in the basic doctrines of Christianity before admission to communicant membership in a church" (*Webster's Seventh New Collegiate Dictionary* definition) as a term for preconfirmation children.

EARLY ADOLESCENCE (AGES 12–16). From the good feelings about themselves of later childhood, girls and boys are plunged into the often turbulent years of adolescence. Physical changes are greeted with both eagerness and trepidation. Sudden growth spurts make these young people feel awkward. Their physical changes also bring about important changes in social relationships with the opposite sex. Peer groups become more important than ever. Being "different" from the group assumes catastrophic proportions: "But, Mom, *everyone* has one!"

Relationships with adults also change in this period. There is tension in relation to parents or guardians as these young people alternate—sometimes with unbelievable rapidity—between wanting more freedom and more opportunities to make decisions for themselves, and falling back into childish dependency. Both boys and girls develop crushes on teachers or athletes or rock stars or other older youth and adults.

During this period these young people begin to ask serious questions about themselves and to make life decisions and commitments. They are apt to be quite idealistic, to dream big dreams, but the dreams are rooted in realism. They know that the longest journey starts with the first step. For the church, this is an important stage, as this is the time when many of these young people commit themselves to Christ and his church through confirmation or joining the church or baptism (if they have not been baptized in infant years).

Intellectually, early adolescents are moving into adult modes of thought. They can put together their observations and perceptions in logical sequence and hypothesize about these in abstract terms. They are adept at problem solving. These abilities make it possible for young people to delve meaningfully into the biblical story. One group of seventh- and eighth-graders decided that to be well-informed Christians they needed to know: (1) How the geography of the Near East and the political history of the area influenced the development of biblical history; (2) How the concepts of God and worship developed and changed from the early concepts of the Old Testament to those held by Christians of New Testament times; (3) How Bible stories, especially the miracle stories, square with scientific knowledge. That agenda would floor most adult Christians, but these young people worked hard for eight months to find answers to their questions.

OLDER YOUTH (AGES 16–22). Most young people in this older group have come to terms with the physical growth and adjustments of early adolescence. They now develop a great surge of vitality and power. They "can do all things." Their idealism and belief in their abilities to achieve whatever they think is good know few bounds because they lack experience with the realities and problems of the adult world. Listen to the sermons they give on Youth Sunday. They are full of enthusiasm, high ideals and a certain amount of condescension or even condemnation for the older generation that has not cured the particular problems they are addressing. But the older generation listens to these sermons because they, too, believe that perhaps this new generation will be able to do the things the older generations dreamed of when they were this age. Because of their idealism, teenagers are often misused by politicians, organizations, even religious leaders to advance particular causes.

For some young people the movement into experiences of the adult world begins early in this period as they leave school to work or to raise a family. For other young women and men, facing up to the hard problems of life is postponed while they are completing their education—sometimes well into the period of young adulthood.

During this period, relationships with peers become all-important. In search of selfhood (identity), young people either commit themselves to sharing their lives with others—their mates, their friends, the Christian fellowship—or they turn away from their peers and become alienated or isolated. They may also be swallowed up by their peers—lose their individual identity within the group as has happened to many who have joined communes or drifted into the drug culture.

Churches concerned for the whole person need to encourage young people to think for themselves, to question the opinions of others, to gather practical experience. In these ways we can help our young men and women to be prepared for the realities of the world. In actual experience the problems they were formerly able to deal with on an idealistic basis now demand rethinking in terms of interlocking with other problems. Compromise is often necessary as the young people discover that others have differing opinions and ideals.

In many ways this is a dangerous period. As young people come face to face with problems beyond their ability to solve, they may fall into the trap of becoming fanatics or carping critics or revolutionaries with no positive contributions to make. Fortunately, most young people avoid this trap, and many find ways to work effectively along with others who are concerned with the same social or religious problems that call for change.

YOUNG ADULTHOOD (AGES 22–28). The major tasks of young adulthood are to make decisions about vocation, marriage or singleness, raising a family; to learn to accept being both dependent and independent in relation to family and friends; to develop a satisfactory philosophy of life. In this period young adults are developing abilities to face reality head-on; to become responsible citizens, workers, family members, church workers; and to participate responsibly in a variety of groups.

The church's educational ministries must serve the many needs of young adults. Participating with older adults in discussion groups dealing with major issues will help the young people express some of their frustrations and help them gain from the experiences of others. For young marrieds the church needs to provide counseling, prenatal classes for adjustments to family life and care of babies (if this is not done by other groups in the community), and programs for families with young children. Young people who decide against marriage need help in developing full lives with relationships that provide affection, acceptance, and companionship; they need opportunities for developing social and personal achievement. It is important to involve members of this age group in all areas of church life, especially to include them on decision-making boards and committees.

MIDDLE ADULTHOOD (AGES 28–65). Analysts differ about both the starting and ending points of middle adulthood. Generally, however, these are the years characterized by occupational development (whether in work outside or within the home), rearing and launching children, investment in community and church responsibilities, and facing the realities of physical changes that lessen physical stamina as persons move into older adulthood.

Much of personal identity during these years is related to persons' work. Persons who do not find satisfying work opportunities or those who become unemployed—including women whose work has been raising a family and who suddenly have no more children at home—may face major identity crises. The church can play an important role in helping these persons find other, satisfying outlets for their abilities. One church with many unemployed members organized a group for these people. At their meetings the members of the group shared their experiences and helped each other think through what alternative lines of work they might enter. The sharing of problems helped these persons to accept themselves and their own problems, and the advice given one another enabled many of the members to go out and work in areas they had never before considered.

A great many people in the middle adult years find real fulfillment in volunteer work beyond their bread-and-butter jobs. Such volunteer work is often an outgrowth of participation in action/reflection groups in the church through which group members have become acquainted with needs of the community and the world and the mandate of the gospel to minister to those in need.

Churches are also incorporating in their educational programs opportunities for persons in middle adulthood to prepare for aging and retirement. Sometimes this subject is included in intergenerational groups using a resource such as *Understanding Aging* (A Shalom Resource, United Church Press), which was written as a study unit for older children but has proved valuable when adults and young people use it together.

These are also the years of maturity when men and women dig deeply into their faith understandings, when the biblical story of God's love can be put together in its fullness.

As with persons of all ages, middle adults continue to struggle with moral values, exploring them in the context of the many violations that occur in personal, social, civic, and international life. These ethical dilemmas can often best be faced in study and discussion groups in which the members have developed enough trust in one another to share their problems honestly and, together, seek a Christian perspective for dealing with the problems.

OLDER ADULTHOOD (AGES 65 AND UP). How persons have experienced and dealt with the processes of living from infancy to age sixty-five will be reflected in their living of their final years. Those who have experienced love and fulfillment and have been able to face disillusionment, sorrow, and problems of various kinds will be able to move into the later years with acceptance of dependence caused by failing strength and physical disabilities. Others who have not achieved as great a sense of wholeness may have a harder time as they lose old friends and perhaps a spouse, face the fact that they cannot achieve some of their hopes and dreams, move to unfamiliar surroundings, become more dependent on younger persons, try to live on a more modest income, and the like.

The most pressing concern in older adulthood is preparing for impending death. The church has a major responsibility for helping persons in this older age group to clarify their beliefs and strengthen their faith so as to enable them to live and die in peace.

These are, or can be, full and exciting years. Older people in good health have more freedom from the world of work and raising a family. They can enter into new and rewarding relationships with their grown children, and happy relations with grandchildren. They can pursue old or new hobbies and interests for which they did not have time earlier. They can form new friendships in new settings. The church can provide many opportunities for older adults to give of their experience and expertise and to enter into new experiences. Even planning one's funeral can be a fulfilling experience. One minister encourages members of his congregation (of all ages) to make such plans. This gives a great opportunity for the minister and the other person to discuss their mutual beliefs and faith, to think about the meaning of eternal life. Together they discuss prayers, Bible passages, hymns, and make decisions about what they want used in funeral or memorial services. The minister provides forms for persons who wish to will parts of their bodies to eye banks and the like. The minister keeps the results of these planning sessions in a file so that when the person dies many of the related details can be taken care of quickly and in fulfillment of the wishes of the deceased.

Thus we see that the church has an educational ministry to persons from birth to death. The whole church teaches and the whole person learns. What is learned, and how it is learned, varies with the development of each person, but churches can make general assumptions and plan educational programs with a good degree of probability of meeting the needs of all persons.

THE IMPORTANCE OF DEVELOPMENTAL STAGES. None of the stages we have been describing begins on a particular birthday and is completed on another birthday in the future. Birth to death is a continuum with continuous development, but it is not a steady line. Some persons may move rapidly through some developmental stages and slowly through others, or progress may be rapid in physical development and slower in cognitive development or vice versa. The value of having an understanding of the basic developmental pattern is that it can guide us in planning our educational ministries in relation to the general interests, abilities and needs of the persons in our churches.

THE SCHOOL OF THE CHURCH
Whatever your church believes about what education is needed, what should be taught, when, and to whom, a major unit in planned educational ministries is usually the church school. Church school classes may be held on Sunday or during the week, or a combination of both. The school may be organized in graded classes, interest groups, or broadly-graded or intergenerational groupings. It may use traditional teaching methods or the learning center approach or an action/reflection approach. The variations are countless. The basic concern, however, is to provide appropriate educational opportunities for all persons in the parish.

SETTINGS FOR PLANNED EDUCATION. Churches need to take a close look at the tradition of Sunday morning church school. In some areas Sunday is still the best time. It is a convenient time for all members of the family to go to church together. For others, this is a poor time. Families go away for the weekend; young people are out late Saturday nights, dating or babysitting; children resent having to get dressed up to go to church on one of their "days off" from school; people who work on Saturdays want to sleep late and have a leisurely day.

Many churches have experimented with both alternative church school programs and services of worship. One church in a predominantly Jewish community finds that Friday afternoon and evening is the best time for their people. School-age children come directly from school for an hour of fun and refreshments followed by classes. Young people come at five for classes. At 6:30 there is a potluck dinner for everyone, followed by a family service of worship. Some adults stay on for study groups and the young people have their fellowship group. This church also has a Sunday morning service with church school for younger children.

A number of churches have weekday afternoon or early evening church school programs. In one suburban area, three churches (of different denominations) share in a common education program. Nursery and kindergarten classes are held in the mornings and afternoons with classes for parents simultaneously. Babysitting service is provided for infants and toddlers. Primary grades meet on one afternoon after school and junior grades on another. Youth and adult groups meet in the evenings of their choice. The advantage of this program for these churches is that the members of the professional staffs (three ministers and two directors of education) are available to do much of the teaching along with volunteer teachers.

A church in Minnesota has been having great success with what they call the Beehive program. Children come to the Beehive for five hours one Saturday a month. This solid block of study and recreational activities enables much more learning and fellowship to occur than is possible in one-hour segments once a week for four or five weeks. Parents, teachers, and other adults meet on Thursday evening prior to the Saturday Beehive for study and preparation on the theme for the Beehive. Youth and adults also have rap sessions before or after the Sunday morning service, and the youth have weekday confirmation classes.

Still other churches utilize weekend retreats for teaching/learning opportunities. In some cases these retreats are for young people only. In other situations whole families participate with age-group and intergenerational groupings and activities. One church reports doing all its planned school in bimonthly weekend retreats plus special all-church study series during Advent and Lent. These series start with a simple meal at 5:00 P.M. and end by or before 8:00 P.M. so that even young children can participate.

Still other churches are experimenting with integrated Sunday morning worship-education-celebration. One pattern is a short, traditional service of worship followed by a variety of educational offerings. Some youth and adults join in discussion of the sermon with the minister. Other adults, children, and young people engage in mission outreach activities. Age-group classes using denominational curriculum are also available for children and youth, and study groups for adults. At the end of the education period, everyone meets together for a brief celebration of their experiences and their life and work together.

No matter how innovative the churches have been in making educational programs and services of worship available to their people at convenient times, most of the churches still have both a service of worship and at least a modified church school on Sunday morning for those who prefer this schedule. Also, the educational opportunities of the church school are usually augmented with vacation church school, special study action groups, camping programs, and other educational ministries in youth and adult fellowship groups.

GROUPING AND GRADING. How the church school is organized depends on the number enrolled, the available space and leadership and the type of program. A small church school will probably organize on a broadly-graded or intergenerational plan in order to have enough persons to make workable groups. "Two's company and three's a crowd," but it takes four and preferably more to make a group. The groups are organized according to the developmental abilities discussed previously. But churches should remain flexible. For example, one year it might be wise to keep the one or two first-graders with the kindergartners; another year, when there are more younger children and fewer older children, the first-graders might be included with second- and third-graders. If the emphasis is on fellowship and working together rather than on grade, there will not be feelings of being "kept back" or "jumped ahead." Churches with only two or three children per grade often use the learning center approach to combine groups of fifteen to thirty children or young people.

Two frequently-used broad gradings are:

I	II
Infants and Toddlers	Infants through age 3
Ages 3–6 (first grade)	Ages 4–7 (second grade)
Grades 2–5	Grades 3–7
Grades 6–8	Grades 8–12
Grades 9–12	All older youth and adults
Older youth and young adults	
Middle and older adults	

The most frequent use of intergenerational groupings is with youth and adults, especially senior high students and adults. But some churches have had good experiences having people of all ages engaged in common learning opportunities. Usually in this type of group the participants spend part of the time together and part of the time working in smaller groups, either by age level or by interest.

Church schools with enrollments of 75 or more are likely to organize on either group grading or close grading. Close grading provides a class for each age level through junior or senior high school. Older youth and adults, and sometimes high school young people, are often organized in a variety of study groups (electives). Group grading, like broad grading, should be flexible to reflect the changing numbers enrolled and the general educational level of the students in relation to the resources chosen; that is, curriculum designed for an average age level development may be too sophisticated for some groups and not advanced enough for others. An average-level group might combine grades four and five, for example. If the students were above average, third and fourth grades might be grouped together using the fourth- and fifth-grade resources. A less advanced group might again have third and fourth grades together but would use materials designed for grades two and three. On the basis of general developmental growth, the following grouping is usually effective:

Infants and toddlers

Ages 3 and 4

Kindergarten and Grade 1 (First-graders are just learning to read and write and are closer to kindergartners than to second-graders in their skills, thought processes and interests.)

Grades 2–3

Grades 4–5

Grades 6–7
Grades 8–9
Grades 10–12
Older youth and single young adults (Older youth through
older adults may be organized on the basis of subject or
interest areas rather than on age.)
Young adults
Middle adults
Older adults

TEACHING

Teaching/learning is a continuous process because teachers are
learners also. But teaching is a special and very important part of
that process. We can get a good picture of the role of the teacher
by looking at the various titles given to persons who teach:

Leaders—those who lead or guide others in a common journey
of exploration and discovery.

Enablers—those who help others along the paths of learning,
raising questions, suggesting various approaches to finding
out what the students want to know.

Facilitators—those who ease the task of learning by providing
resources and helping each student find the best way for her
or him to pursue a task.

Teachers (the term as used in a limited way)—those who in-
struct and aid students in the learning process with planned
resources and learning activities.

Lecturers—those who provide input of ideas and information
and stimulate thinking.

Good teachers combine all these roles. They not only open
doors, they lead their students in exploratory paths. They equip
their pupils with resources to help them explore and discover.
They plan learning activities that enable students to make discoveries and to put their findings together in ways that help the students to conceptualize and comprehend their learnings and act
upon them.

Teachers are also sometimes called *managers* of learning.
Note that we say managers of learn*ing*, not of learn*ers*.

SETTING GOALS AND OBJECTIVES

Managers, whether in a factory or in a church education program,
are responsible for determining what needs to be accomplished

and how. Determining what needs to be accomplished in Christian education is another way of deciding what doors we hope to open and what we hope will be explored and discovered as students venture through them. It makes no difference whether we call this door-opening plan *goals* or *aims* or *purposes*. The important task is to know where one hopes to go in a course, in a unit, in a session, in a particular activity. An intriguing book title reads: If You Don't Know Where You're Going, You'll Probably End Up Somewhere Else.

SAMPLE GOALS. A nursery teacher might have as a goal: "To enable students to learn about God's love as they experience love and friendship in their church group."

Teachers of fifth- or sixth-graders might aim during a course or unit: "To explore the biblical story of the liberation of the Hebrews from slavery in Egypt and how we can help liberate oppressed people today."

Leaders of a youth or adult group might have as their purpose for one or more sessions: "To get reports on needs of the elderly people in our community and to plan an action project to help them meet those needs."

Setting objectives involves determining what portion or aspect of the goal (purpose, aim) is to be accomplished in a given time span or situation. The teachers of juniors studying the exodus might set as their objective for one session: To tell and dramatize the story of Moses' pleading with Pharaoh so that the students will be able to recall what Moses asked and how the Pharaoh responded.

The best-planned goals and objectives of teachers can fall flat if they are not shared by the students. The teaching team of a junior high class was about to give up on the goal of enabling the students to put together the Bible story. But the teachers hit upon the idea of asking the students what they thought they should know about the Bible in order to be able to tell non-Christians about it. The students came up with an amazing list, and worked harder than ever before to learn what *they felt* they needed to know.

It is relatively easy for younger children to share in the goals and objectives set by the teacher. These children are eager to learn, and seldom question the rightness of adult choices. This thesis does break down at times. Children in early and middle childhood, for example, get very excited about Halloween, and the teacher who tries to ignore this important event and continue "business as usual" is in for some frustrating sessions. Wise teachers enlarge or adapt their goals and objectives to include making Halloween decoration or preparing children to collect for UNICEF as part of their trick-or-treat fun.

A junior class politely went along with the adult-set goal of "exploring the meaning of 'In the beginning God created. . . .'" The children enjoyed the nature hike, making collages with their findings, and examining rock and shell collections. But they did not get excited about the goal and make it their own until they got into a discussion of how the world *really* got created—according to science and, interestingly, in light of their extensive knowledge of science fiction. The *Planet of the Apes* was more real to this group than the biblical story of creation. This discussion opened the door for their questions and wonderings, and helped the teachers to modify their goals and objectives to join with their students in a common search for understanding of religious and scientific concepts of creation.

LEARNING ACTIVITIES

Once goals and objectives have been set, taking into account both the subject area and the students' interests and needs, the next step in the teaching/learning process is to plan ways to accomplish these purposes. What learning activities will most effectively help students move through the doors and explore the area beyond? We have three guides in making our selections: (1) the content of the subject area; (2) the developmental stage of the students; (3) the setting or environment. Learning activities chosen for a weekend retreat setting will probably be quite different from those chosen for a Sunday or weekday church school session even if the subject area is the same.

GROUP-BUILDING ACTIVITIES. Regardless of age, people find it difficult to share at any depth until a sense of community and a sense of trust have been established. This may mean postponing major work on the subject area in favor of get-acquainted games or activities that will build rapport.

INQUIRY-EXPLORING ACTIVITIES. Students need information and opportunities to explore ideas and concepts. With younger age groups inquiry-exploring activities include storytelling, looking at pictures, manipulating objects (blocks, puzzles, toys), dressing up, playing house and the like. Older age groups may do guided Bible or other study; use books, films, filmstrips to do research; raise questions and seek answers through interviews, field trips, experimentations, games or other modes of inquiry.

EXPRESSIVE-CELEBRATIVE ACTIVITIES. These activities enable students to put together the information and ideas they have been exploring. Such activities include drama, art and building projects, creative writing, worship experiences, making reports, keeping records, singing, dancing. By giving form to their findings, the students are expressing what the content means to them. Such activities also serve to reinforce the learnings.

ACTION ACTIVITIES. These may precede or follow other kinds of activities. Action may reveal to students the information they need in order to act more effectively. Or, action may lead to reflection on biblical or other material. For example, a group may be concerned about prison reform. They get into action by taking a field trip to a prison, taking gifts for the prisoners. At the prison they learn firsthand of the needs of the people and the problems they are facing. This leads to further action of involving the whole church in working for prison reform and to adopting the prison the group visited as a special mission project.

RECALL AND "CATCH-UP" ACTIVITIES. The biggest problems in planned programs of Christian education are the length of time between sessions, and absenteeism. Except for retreats or vacation church school, most educational programs have meetings once a week at best, whether the meetings are on Sunday or a weekday. It is usually necessary to spend a few minutes recalling what the group was doing at the last session. This may be done by reading any record made by the group, looking at projects under way and recalling what was done and what next steps need to be taken, or by verbal recall by students present at the previous session. This recall also enables persons who were absent to get "clued in." If work is being done on individual projects, the former absentees may be given a modified version of the project to do so that they may catch up with the rest of the group.

GETTING THE MOST FROM LEARNING ACTIVITIES. Many years of study have shown that persons learn most when the largest number of their senses and abilities are involved. This confirms the old saying that "experience is the best teacher." The least involvement, and therefore the lowest rate of learning, usually occurs when persons just listen. If we want to reclaim education for the church, we must use teaching/learning activities that *insofar as possible involve the whole person in the action.* Different persons learn differently. Some learn best with verbal activities: reading or listening. Others learn best through activities involving use of the hands.

Using a variety of learning activities may be an uncomfortable approach for teachers who have relied heavily on lecture or reading the lesson material aloud and asking questions about the lesson. Students with good memories will learn something good about the content of such lessons. Others are apt to forget what they heard or read as soon as they leave. But taking the time and making the effort to use more activities can bring rich rewards.

One teacher reluctantly agreed to have her seventh-grade students build a relief map of the Near East as an activity to help the girls and boys learn about the impact of geography on Hebrew history. It seemed to her a waste of time until the Sunday one boy burst into class exclaiming: "Guess what! We studied Palestine in school this week, and I could tell them it was a real place!" (Obviously the reference must have been to a history lesson as there is no "Palestine" today.) This boy had been in church school for nine years and had heard many Bible stories but it was not until he did the research and helped build the map that he realized that Palestine was a real place and that the people of the Bible were real persons. The teacher suddenly realized that through this involving activity the students had learned for themselves what she could have told them a dozen times without their making connections. She shared the joy of the boy and vowed that in the future she would use whatever activities would best help her students truly to learn.

TIME FOR TEACHING

Using good learning activities takes time, and volunteer teachers seldom have a lot of time to give to teaching in church education programs. Good teaching, however, need not take much more time than poor teaching! The secret is to take an extra hour or two *at the beginning* of each course and unit to discover what it is about—what the goals and objectives are, what activities are suggested for learning, what story and other resources are available. Knowing where you are going and what resources will help you get there is half the job done. Session by session preparation can then be done in an hour or so each week.

Of course, really good teachers spend more time than an hour in preparation but that is because they think about the students and about the sessions at odd moments while going to or from their work, or while doing chores around the house. One excellent teacher found that she did most of her preparation while doing her weekly ironing. She skimmed through the session outline and suggested resources before starting to iron, then kept a pad of paper and pencil handy to jot down ideas that occurred to her as she worked. Another teacher both consciously and subconsciously looks for cartoons, pictures, stories and articles related to the subject of his course as he reads the papers and his magazines. When the time comes to outline their sessions these teachers have most of the work done. If activities they plan to use require extra resources, they pick these up here and there as they go about their work so that the day before the session does not find them rushing around trying to gather everything they need.

Finally, good teachers plan to be in their classrooms or meeting places a good half hour before time for starting the session. This gives them time to get materials out and the space arranged to say to the arriving students: "Welcome! We are ready for you. Something interesting is going to happen here today. Come in and join us."

Teachers who arrive with their students, or after their students, are in effect saying to their students: "You, and what we will be doing here today, are not really important enough for me to bother about getting here early to get ready for you." These teachers are teaching their students that Christian education and the church and God and Jesus Christ are not very important, not as important as an extra half hour of sleep or watching television or reading the papers or whatever. Christian education cannot be reclaimed unless Christians and churches are willing to give it high priorities in their lives.

MOTIVATION FOR LEARNING

Contrary to what many children and young people would like to make us believe, most of them *like* to learn. What they don't like is to be bored, to have their interests ignored, to be poured into a mold, to be forced to abide by someone else's agenda.

A number of churches have been using the learning center approach in their church schools, and most have reported increased interest and attendance because this approach provides a variety of learning opportunities and allows students to have a larger part in selecting what and how they will learn, thus providing greater motivation. (See *Guidelines to the Learning Center Approach in Church Education,* $1.25; and *The Learning Center Revisited,* $1.50, available from DECEE, Box 179, St. Louis, Missouri, 63166.)

A church in Oregon held interviews with children, youth and adults to determine what *they* thought about the educational program of the church. The education committee also studied books on various educational approaches. The result was the development of a new program something like the Beehive program described earlier. Parents, teachers, and other adults met with the minister for study and preparation related to the theme of the church school, and the church school met after school on a weekday in a modified learning center program. There was no lack of motivation for learning as the children built a Palestinian house large enough to get into, built a Palestinian oven, and developed other projects, all the time learning about life in Palestine in Bible times and about some of the biblical persons.

It has been proved over and over again that when someone's interest is captured, that person will put forth immense effort to learn as much about the subject as possible. A seven-year-old astounded his parents and teachers by his vast knowledge of astronomy. He spent hours pouring over encyclopedias and books on astronomy, all on his own. In all other respects he was an average child, but someone had "turned him on" to astronomy.

In our planned Christian education we need to do our best to capture our students' interests. This does not mean that we do not sometimes work in areas of less interest to the students, but we try to approach our teaching in such a way that the students will be willing to share the teachers' concerns. Most students are fair if we will meet them half way.

The use of rewards, other than genuine appreciation of the person and his or her work, usually indicates poor teaching/learning. It means that we feel we have to bribe students to come and to learn. The trouble with such bribes is that we can't keep them up forever, and many students drop out when the bribes stop because their motivation for coming is gone.

The best rewards for most of us are a sense of accomplishment and a word of appreciation or congratulation from other persons. Sometimes a smile or a hug or a pat is all that is needed to encourage persons to dig into a job that they do not like or that seems too big. A sense of humor helps also.

We need to check our planned educational programs to see how they relate to the persons in those programs—and persons that we wish were in the programs—and what needs to be done to motivate learning more effectively. Perhaps churches need to let the children and young people in their church schools know that what the students are doing is important to the whole church. Opportunities may be provided when students of whatever age share their work with the whole church. This may be done through participation in the service of worship as individuals, or groups may share prayers they have written, do a choric reading, sing a special song, or do a rhythmic interpretation of a scripture passage. At other times the students may share what they have done during the coffee hour.

One church has monthly "sit-down" coffees for reports of various kinds, including sharing by church school classes. At one such sit-down coffee the learning center group (grades one through five) showed a film they had made of the Good Samaritan story, followed by a UNICEF film. They then invited the people to fish in two fish-ponds the children had prepared to raise money for UNICEF. The children had made many of the prizes for which the people fished. The money raised was added to the amounts that had been collected for UNICEF during their Halloween trick-or-treat rounds for a total of $87, a good-sized amount for a group of eighteen children to raise. There was plenty of motivation for studying the biblical parable and for working to help their needy neighbors today. The reward of satisfaction for a job well done, plus plenty of praise and cooperation from the adults, made this a memorable learning experience.

Church school students can also be involved in all-church projects. As they share in planning and action they may grow in self-respect—"I'm doing something important"—and at the same time develop feelings of belonging.

We all need memorable learning experiences. These are the bases of learnings that will contribute to helping the church continue, today, tomorrow, and in the twenty-first century. The church lives through the people who are joyously committed to Christ and the working of the Holy Spirit in the world.

WHAT WE BELIEVE ABOUT CHRISTIAN EDUCATION

In this chapter we have been discussing teaching/learning as inseparable, ongoing processes by which people are enabled to move toward commitment to God and the church. What are the concepts of teaching/learning held by the members of your congregation? What would they say are the goals and objectives for Christian education? What subject areas do they think should be studied in the planned education program? A church concerned with reclaiming Christian education as a basic function of the church must answer these questions before it can construct a viable program.

Questions such as the above should be discussed by the whole congregation. If this is not feasible, questionnaires can be used and the results checked by the consistory or church council or an education committee and then reported to the congregation. An effective questionnaire is in itself a teaching and learning resource. A variety of statements about Christian education can be listed, and persons asked to rank the statements in order of importance. Some of the statements may be new ideas for some of the people and will challenge their thinking. Statements might be drawn from this book, from *The Educational Mission of Our Church* by Roger Shinn (United Church Press), from *Guidelines for Evaluating Christian Education in the Local Church* (United Church Press), and other educational resources.

But what if the congregation has rather rigid, narrow concepts of Christian education? Does this say that the church has to have a rigid, narrow educational program? No. It does mean, however, that the first step to be taken by those concerned with a broader, more open and fruitful program of Christian education is to educate the congregation. This can be done in sermons by the minister, in articles in the church newsletter, in small study groups, in programs in adult fellowship groups, and the like. Then effective educational ministries can be developed and implemented gradually. The results will be an improvement over what the situation was in the past. They can even revitalize the whole church!

CHAPTER 5

ELEMENTS TO BE CONSIDERED: RESOURCES AND PROCEDURES

1. KNOW THE PEOPLE

Earlier we said, "Changing thinking, feeling, intentions, and actions is one way to describe what learning and teaching are all about."* Education in the church is one way of helping people change and grow as Christians. To develop an effective Christian education program requires that we know the people who will be involved. It also requires that educational plans be designed to meet the needs of people, rather that expecting people to participate in a program just because it is offered. Knowing the people in your church, therefore, is essential.

The first question to ask is: Who are in the congregation? (Data about age groupings is important.)

Information such as the following will prove useful:
a. How many preschool children?_____
b. How many elementary schoolage children?
   Children ages 6—8_____
   Children ages 9—11 _____
c. How many junior high (or middle school) young people?
   _____ What are their ages?_____
d. How many younger teens (high school)? _____
e. How many older teens—college and/or employed? _____
f. How many young adults under 30? _____
g. How many adults in 30s to 50s? _____
h. How many adults in 50s and 60s? _____
i. How many persons in older years? _____

Why such data? Because types of programs are often determined by the available customers! For example, many small churches may have only a few children, perhaps fifteen to twenty, in all the elementary grades. Divided into age level classes, there are too few for lively groups and stimulating interchange among persons. But such small groupings, and also situations with 40 or

---

*Page 25.

50 or more, offer excellent opportunities for a learning center approach style of church school work. The minister of such a church once described his church situation in a tone of despair. "We have just one big room in the basement," he said, "and a handful of kindergartners, with about thirty grade school children. It's really rough putting a class in each corner, with one group out in the middle of the floor. No one wants to teach with all that confusion."

The counselor with whom he was talking asked the minister to draw a rough sketch of the room. He did so. Then the counselor pointed out the possibility of using learning centers, and went over the curriculum resource materials to show the minister how they might be adapted to provide content for several learning centers that could be used by various ages. The change was made after careful planning, and the church school took on new life.

The data on who was in the church at elementary school age level made the difference between struggling along with a teaching/learning structure that was unsuitable and ineffective, and experimenting with a more flexible alternative that still provided sound educational opportunities for the children. Knowing the people and taking their needs into account, was the key to improvement in design.

In another kind of situation, an intergenerational series of discussion-study groups proved the best option when a Christian education committee faced the fact that eight high school young people, four out-of-school young adults, and several young married couples were all interested in discovering what their church could do about a rising crime problem in their neighborhood. Numbers in each age group were such that separate programs would have lacked vigor. Together, the group met with community leaders, studied the biblical perspective on justice, and got into action by persuading the church council to make the church building regularly available for community experiences such as AA meetings, a neighborhood craft center, a weekly gathering for elderly residents and those in a nursing home who were able on occasion to visit outside, and a club center for teenagers.

Churches in a mountain town of 10,000 learned from declining enrollment in the traditional summer vacation school that this two-week program lacked interest for children. Leadership was also growing harder to recruit. Four downtown churches got together and canvassed the situation. Both children and youth wanted to be outdoors and wanted variety in what they did during the summer. As a result of this information, a new type of summer experience was planned called Summer Ecumenical Experience (SEE). Each Wednesday was scheduled for two full summer months as a one-day-a-week outdoor-oriented educational ministry. All children and youth in the community were welcome. A team of lay persons and ministers took responsibility for planning and carrying out each week.

Trips to various points of interest, hikes, nature study including the biblical point of view of nature, creative crafts, participating in community projects, helping persons in need were some of the activities. Adults were very willing to spend one day a week once or twice during the summer instead of feeling "saddled" with a solid two-week stretch of time. The churches learned new values for their educational ministries from these outdoor-oriented experiences. And the young people were so enthusiastic at having something special to do once a week all summer that Wednesdays became popularly known throughout the community as SEE days. Something new had been found that helped churches meet needs of children, young people, and adults.

A second question is: what are the interests, skills, and concerns of the people? Many churches have sent out questionnaires to members asking for such information as:

a. What concerns of yours are not being dealt with in the various congregational activities?

b. What do you like best, or have found most helpful, in what is being offered?

c. In what kind of church activities will you participate?

d. What would you be willing to do to help in the church life, especially the educational program?

Response to questionnaires is seldom 100 percent; often considerably less. But response itself is a clue to interest and willingness to participate.

Another kind of questionnaire may list all the present education activities—both those with a primary educational focus (church school, adult study groups), and those with another primary focus but with by-product educational results (choir, special seasonal events, worship). Members are asked to check those in which they participate, to evaluate activities (using such a rating as 1 for very helpful, 2 for moderately helpful, 3 for uninteresting), and then either to list, or check on a prepared list, the subjects, activities or needs they would like to see dealt with in the educational life of the church.

Skills of people may also be learned by questionnaires, or by interviews, or simply by observation.

Such skills ought to be kept on a record card, perhaps the person's church membership card. Some people are glad to use professional skills, such as teaching; others prefer to work in something they don't do all week long. Knowing people as persons—not alone as names and information on a card—is extremely important in becoming aware of talent, and how people are willing to use theirs. It is equally important to know which persons are also genuinely participating in the life of the church simply by being faithful attenders, but who, for reasons of time or other personal considerations, may be unable to do more.

There is no substitute for knowing the people, who they are, what they like, what they think they need. Whether the church is large or small, making such acquaintance is a time-consuming process at some points; but it is a personally rewarding one in its potential for helping the education committee design and carry out education that is meaningful and that genuinely helps to communicate the faith and to involve people in living it.

A subcommittee of the Christian education committee may take responsibility for initiating the process of discovering the best ways to know the people. In such work, however, the diaconate or consistory, board of parish services, and other boards ought to be equally involved, as, of course, should the clergy and other church staff. Knowing the people is a shared activity that lays foundations for a wholistic approach to church life in its totality, and education is a contributioon to it. Each board or group will bring special perspective and concerns that, when put together, produce a wholistic search for, and use of, talents of church members.

2. DECIDE WHO IS RESPONSIBLE

We all know that Christian education—even the simple step of filling out an order blank for resource materials—doesn't just happen in a congregation. People—one person or a group of persons—have to be responsible for seeing that a job is done. In developing a Christian education program from a wholistic approach reliable, enthusiastic, committed people are essential for two kinds of responsibilities: for planning and designing the total educational program, and for managing and supervising the work as it is implemented or carried out. Planning, designing, and implementing are all part of a whole, and are interrelated, but must be considered separately at the start. Continuing attention must be given to each of these parts of the total educational program once they are developed, if the program is to be effective. The same, of course, is true of every other part of the congregation's life. No effective comprehensive program can be started, then left to run by itself.

Who, then, are possibilities for "being responsible"? There are several. We may think of the pastor, of the educational board or committee, and of the congregation itself.

Let's examine each of these carefully, beginning with the one mentioned last. Certain kinds of responsibility belong to each.

THE CONGREGATION
Obviously the entire congregation cannot be expected to assume the designing and implementing responsibility. But each member of the congregation does have a responsibility to support the educational program. Support includes affirming the program, or offering constructive criticism of it, and sharing in developing goals for the church that include educational ones. Support also includes participating in educational opportunities that are offered. Some members may participate only in events that appeal to their particular interests or needs. All members can share in total church events that have educational implications or content.

For example, just before Advent in one church the young people developed a play they called "What's Happening to God's World?" The drama was the outgrowth of several weekend retreat trips to ecological, industrial and art centers in the surrounding area. In the play the youth expressed personal questions about faith in today's world that had arisen during their times together. At the end of the play, they invited their friends in the church to join them in two-way conversation about appropriate answers to these questions.

The young people asked permission to present their play sometime during Advent. The pastor and church council approved making the play the sermon for the second Sunday in Advent. In fact, its length made it the feature of the entire order of service, so hymns, prayers, and scripture were chosen accordingly. Attendance at that service was considerably smaller than on the first or third Sundays in Advent in that church. Many older people, as well as a number of younger people, stayed away. Why? When asked, a number of them gave answers such as "That was just for youth and their parents" or "I want to hear a sermon, not a youth program."

This congregation seemed only partially to support and understand what education, teaching and learning are. The stay-aways may have viewed the youth and their play as a performance, not a faith expression and a learning occasion for the congregation.

In another church, by contrast, the children and junior highs in the church school also worked out a play, growing out of their fall study of worship. During the same period senior highs and adults had also been studying worship in their own intergenerational group. "Why not?" was the church council's response when it was suggested that the play, "Looking for a Star," be the heart of the service on the first Sunday in Advent. So it was. And the junior choir with Adam (mentioned earlier) replaced the adult choir for the morning. The congregation smiled sympathetically at a few mishaps in production, and joined heartily in carol singing. After the service, everyone pitched in to hang decorations in the sanctuary, trim the traditional tree, or just join in watching and coffee-ing. This congregation did support education, finding in this Advent celebration another time for learning as a community of faith, along with appreciating what the planned Christian education program was doing in the church.

To be supportive, congregations must be kept informed of what is going on by way of planned Christian education. Inserts in Sunday morning bulletins, vignette reports in church newsletters, posters and announcements on church bulletin boards, lively reports at annual meetings, periodic sharing events are just a few possible ways for helping a congregation know what's going on, and in what they may share corporately and individually, or at home as families. One congregation regularly takes pictures of various educational and other church events, mounts them on a large bulletin board in the main hallway titled "We're Doing This!"—and so reminds the congregation visually of highlights of education, worship, and fellowship.

AN EDUCATIONAL BOARD OR COMMITTEE

By whatever name it may be called, the persons responsible for the basic designing of educational program, and the ongoing supervision and implementation of what is designed, must be a core group recognized officially by the church. Its functions must be clearly assigned and understood.

This may be a board of Christian education or a Christian education committee. Membership on this board or committee should be representative of several groups in the church that can provide settings for educational programs. In smaller churches, the Christian education board might include the church school superintendent, a representative of the youth group, a church-member-at-large, and a church council member. In larger churches such boards may include the church school superintendent, a church school teacher, a member of the diaconate or consistory, a trustee, and two or three persons with special educational interests or other related expertise. The minister usually is an ex-officio member. Membership's interests should represent a diversity of concerns in the congregation, not just those of one educating group such as the church school.

If such a board is large, it may have a small executive group that will meet frequently to evaluate the present, dream of future possibilities, and plot out concerns that the entire board may consider. On the other hand, a smaller board can often meet frequently, so there is no need for an executive group. Whatever the structure, the chairperson is a crucial kind of leader. She or he should be imaginative yet down-to-earth; skilled enough to manage meetings and keep the board's work moving along briskly, yet sensitive about allowing proper amounts of time for agenda items; and able to help everyone feel involved in program designing and decision-making. The chairperson must also be able to see that individual members are assigned specific responsibilities in which each person's particular skills or abilities will be utilized.

The atmosphere of meetings should encourage genuine participation, (which may include vigorous disagreements that must be resolved) with the whole life of the congregation as the context within which plans are being developed and carried out. At the same time, the board must keep specific educational settings in view, such as church school, youth work, confirmation, seasonal events, service opportunities, and the like, together with the range of persons in the congregation and what they need or desire.

A board of Christian education should also work cooperatively with other official church groups. The board may take the lead by suggesting its concern, confer with others about their ideas, and then the groups may together work on the particular program problem. Keeping in touch will enable each group to relate its plans to the other's, and the board of education can work with other groups to take advantage of the by-product or unplanned learning opportunities in events that are not designed primarily as educational. For example, one church in Nebraska says "Our goal is to be a Whole Church, a community of faith that expresses its life and mission wholistically. All committees, organizations and groups study, plan, and act upon common goals arrived at by all participants. All groups focus on those goals when they do program planning. Our planning process includes a theological study to guide us in choosing our style of life and mission."

This church listed these settings in which education is a prime focus: church school; youth and adult confirmation; adult, youth, and children's fellowships; leadership events; retreats and camping; current issues group; a personal growth group; special family events; a Great Books club; and a teenagers group. The Christian education committee is responsible for those settings. Settings whose prime focus was other than educational, but which had some educational results, included the services of worship, council sessions, family discovery ventures, the monthly breakfast on Sunday morning when the whole church gathers, and Shalom events on hunger, peace, and sexuality. Other committees bear responsibility for these settings.

In this church the Christian education committee, the celebration and worship committee, and the church council work together so that both planned educational events and the by-products educational results contribute to the total educational life of the church. Evaluation of this wholeness is made at each annual meeting. Input is also solicited from individual persons through interviews, questionnaires and surveys. As a result, in this particular church the board of education plays a primary role in Christian education events, working with other official groups. Thus, in the long run, the entire congregation contributes through participation and annual goal-setting and evaluation. Shared and coordinated responsibility results in wholeness of total educational life in the church.

In another church, in Minnesota, the pastor was asked, "Who is responsible for overseeing the development of an integrated program of education in the life of your church?" The response was:

"Congregation—clergy—Christian education committee—church council—probably in that order. Feed-in is provided at each step of our development process, and on to the next. Christian education committee members each have responsibility for one phase of each event in which education is a prime responsibility." In this small church all organizational elements work together, but with clear understanding of responsibilities.

THE PASTOR

The pastor is a key person for developing education that is integrated into the whole life of the church. If he or she does not believe in the value of education in the church, both the congregation and church committees, including the board of education, will lack an essential kind of support and encouraging leadership. On the other hand, if the pastor believes that Christian education throughout the congregation's life is a major ministry, then everyone will be affirmatively affected and encouraged by his or her leadership.

The pastor may be the person who takes direct responsibility for guiding development of educational plans and implementation of them. Or, he or she may be the adviser, counselor, suggester of innovations. Certainly she or he should play a major role in helping the congregation develop goals and purposes for their life; educational goals will be among these. Either directly or cooperatively, as the situation warrants, the pastor is overseer of educational development, even though actual ongoing responsibilities rightly rest in the board of Christian education and other church committees.

For example, a pastor in a church in Michigan sensed that things were not going very well in the two church school sessions that met during the period of the two Sunday morning worship services. He encouraged the board of Christian education to evaluate the situation, and begin to do some goal setting. "What do we want to accomplish through our educational work?" was a basic question. A current, widely-read book was used to get wheels turning. It did not provide answers to what to do, but it did start the board to searching for alternative ways of carrying on education on Sunday morning. The board asked the pastor to submit a proposal. He did so; it was not quite the answer either. So he had to go back to the drawing boards for a second and a third time. Finally, after about a year of searching and considering, a "Family Church" program was designed. It included worship and learning centers for all ages, some on an intergenerational basis. This new format was offered during one service only, leaving the second morning period to continue the familiar worship and church school class format. This diversity gave members of the congregation a choice.

In this instance, the pastor carried direct responsibility for helping to develop goals and design and implement program. Actual administration is done by him, with the help of a representative advisory committee chaired by a board member. "It's too bad that I have to take this much direct leadership," he says, "but people are involved and they are learning to take and exercise more responsibility." In time this pastor anticipates being "general overseer" with much more of the basic and specific development responsibilities being taken by members of the board.

A very different situation, in a southern state, confronted a church when the new ministers, a husband and wife team who had been called to the pastorate, arrived. The Sunday school was large and flourishing; it ran parallel to the church worship service. The superintendent had held the position for ten years and had performed administrative duties faithfully. There was no board of education. The Sunday school was considered all that was needed educationally, at least in the feelings of those who attended, especially the adult class.

The new ministers quickly observed, however, that the youth and children's groups were falling off in attendance. There were also other adults who came only to church worship services. Little by little the ministers called on every member of this small parish. At some point they inquired "What does the church hope to accomplish through Christian education?" Few people had ever really thought about that. But the question got people to talking. The role of the Sunday school was looked at, and its opportunities for study and fellowship affirmed. Questions about other educational needs were also heard. Eventually the church council decided that there ought to be a committee which had general oversight of Christian education, including the Sunday school. And so this church started on the road of looking at Christian education from more of a wholistic point of view.

What had the role of the ministers been here? In a quiet but clearly determined way they had helped the church grow in understanding of Christian education. They had helped it get on the path of developing goals and investigating new possibilities.

98

They assumed responsibility for managing, in order to help members of the congregation grow and to pave the way for additional educational opportunities to be built on the foundations already existing. They did not make the mistake of condemning or throwing out what already existed; they saw it as an opportunity for broadening horizons.

The role of the pastor will vary. But the pastor is vital in the development of Christian education from a wholistic point of view. Without his or her active support, the essential interrelationship of pastor, boards and committees, and members of the church will not be present to foster an educational ministry that is soundly grounded in the faith and enables persons to grow in Christian commitment and action.

3. SELECT AND TRAIN LEADERS

In the wholistic perspective for developing a Christian education program in your church, many people can serve as leaders in many different ways. In earlier sections of this book we have spoken of people who design and develop the program. These persons are leaders. The persons who administer, supervise, and evaluate the program are also leaders. Sometimes they are the same persons who did the designing; sometimes they are other people. Then, of course, there are those persons who bear the responsibility for being the teachers who conduct the planned portions of the educational program. In "Identify What We Believe About Education," (see Chapter 4, page 79) you have no doubt already read the list of titles given to persons who teach, and the distinctive characteristics of each: leader, enabler, the facilitator, teacher, lecturer. The good teacher may combine all these roles, as we have already noted, but the distinctive leadership functions are important. In addition to designers, administrators, and teachers, special resource persons should be listed among the kinds of leaders needed for a complete educational ministry. Also important are leaders whose tasks are not primarily educational, such as choir leaders, but whose work has a teaching/learning dimension for people.

SOME GUIDELINES FOR RECRUITING

Clearly, leadership is a shared responsibility in a wholistic educational ministry. How do we go about selecting and recruiting the right kinds of leaders?

Securing the best possible person for each leadership assignment is never easy. The desperate plea "It won't take much work" is a real downgrading of education. Never resort to it! But there are ways of making the task of selection and recruitment easier so there may be confidence that the best persons available have been enlisted.

WHOM DO YOU HAVE? A first step is to examine the total program that has been planned in all parts of the church's life. The design team, or another special corps of people from the board of Christian education, should analyze each planned educational program or event for the kind of leaders required. Look at the number, as well as the style of leadership arrangement required. Some of the possibilities are: a single leader; a team of teachers; a coordinating leader with special resource persons from time to time; specialists in areas such as Bible, archaeology, church and government, the family, or other such concerns; specialists in music to provide choir and instrumental services; a librarian; an educational program secretary for keeping records and handling special arrangements.

Make a chart of the leaders needed. Make it a wall chart that can be kept up and referred to easily. The chart may list both a maximum ideal number of leaders, and a rock bottom minimum.

WHAT ABILITIES ARE REQUIRED? Now identify the characteristics, skills, and abilities especially needed by each leader. The nature of your program units will help you to compile this listing. Keep in mind the need to have both men and women as leaders. One church school noted for its excellent nursery program for three-year-olds attributed a portion of its success to the presence of two men teachers in the teaching team of three, plus musical and art specialists who were on call when needed. Couples have long been known as good possibilities for leaders of both church school and youth groups; the same is becoming true for intergenerational groupings too.

WHO ARE QUALIFIED? When you have completed your chart, including qualifications needed, take a look at the roster of your church membership. In section 1 of this chapter, "Know the People," appear suggested procedures, including possible questionnaires, for discovering just who the people in your church are. In securing this data, provide a place for people to express their

100

interests, describe their backgrounds and skills. This "data bank" can now be drawn upon for matching possible leaders with the positions on your chart. Of course, it is also essential to have some personal knowledge of the individuals in order to know who will be best suited for each position.

HOW AND WHEN SHOULD YOU RECRUIT? After possible matchings have been made, a schedule of personal contacts with the prospective leaders should be drawn up. Decide who will make the contacts. Phoning or personal calling may be used. Select the way of making contacts that will most effectively convey these basic points: a sketch of the total program and its goals; a description of the particular leadership job for which the person is being interviewed and its responsibilities; indication of the time requirements involved; a pledge that the church will make training and equipment available; and the specific length of time for which the leader is being recruited. At all costs avoid the indefinite "for a while" approach; people want to know how long their commitment is—whether for six weeks, four months, a year, or some other period. Above all, convey the sense that the person is being asked to be part of a larger team concerned for sound education in the church in order to help the congregation fulfill its goals and mission.

When should recruiting begin? The best time varies. One church recruits in the spring for fall responsibilities.. This means that designing is completed by late winter for the year beginning in the next fall. Another church, which has a small church school and assorted youth activities, plus informal adult study groups meeting for short terms, seems to operate on a hand-to-mouth basis because people are called in the summer or whenever a new term or interest group surfaces as a live possibility. Actually, this style of operation is not as casual as it seems because the board of Christian education knows the church membership very well, knows who has taught when and whom, what personal family or other plans may be, and the like. The selection of prospects and contacting is done informally, somewhat on a friend to friend basis.

In congregations where people are not so well known personally to each other, even if only a half dozen leadership positions need to be filled, the chart and characteristics of the position idea is a good one to use. Whatever the number of leaders being recruited, the information suggested above ought always to be included as background for the invitation to responsible decision. Such information enhances the significance of educational leadership, and the person is more likely to take the work seriously and see it as a challenging opportunity for both service and personal growth as a Christian.

TRAINING FOR EDUCATIONAL LEADERS

Persons who consent to serve as leaders deserve to receive genuine support from the church. Support includes:

1. resources and equipment adequate to the particular leadership responsibility;
2. opportunities for training in the skills and background needed for the task—Bible, life issues, faith interpretation, age level understanding, methodologies and teaching techniques, and the like;
3. participation in events that give the sense that all the leaders are part of a team;
4. ongoing opportunities for personal enrichment and for experiencing joy and fulfillment in serving as a leader;
5. congregational recognition and expression of appreciation of the leaders and their work.

That's rather a long list, but it's an important one!

Opportunities for training are available in most areas. One task of the board of Christian education is to seek them out and make them available to the leaders. Sometimes individual churches prefer to conduct their own in-service training. Or several churches in a community may join for basic skills, faith interpretation, and other general kinds of training, leaving specialized preparation for local development. Consultants may be engaged for giving specific help to a church in areas such as age level understandings, teaching skills, or overall program development. Area workshops sponsored by denominational agencies are frequently available, sometimes as a several-day workshop, more often as a weekend retreat.

In recent years, groups of leaders in a local church have found it especially rewarding to gather at frequent intervals to share and evaluate their experiences. This, too, is a basic part of training. More than one leader has said, "These mornings (or evenings) together have helped me understand the faith better than anything I've done." At such sessions explicit training in some of the areas mentioned above can be done by use of various media such as tapes or films; reading and discussion; exercises in managing conflict; helping people set their learning goals; learning how persons learn and grow at various age levels, and the like. Planning next steps in each person's area of leadership responsibility, when done together, also creates a sense that "we're all in this together" and provides a greater wealth of possible ways to go about teaching or leading.

Using such group methods to provide training and enrichment will help prevent leaders from feeling "stuck" with a job, or experiencing the desolate sense that "I'm doing this and nobody seems to care what happens."

Taking leaders in groups, or singly, to spend a day in a resource center is another valuable form of offering training and a chance to broaden horizons. More and more such centers are being developed by denominational or interdenominational area agencies, or by individual entrepreneurs who are Christian education specialists. Many resources are on display, to be explored either for specific suggestions or to get broader ideas of what can be done in church education. Such visits are practical, horizon-expanding, and fun times. An experienced Christian educator is usually on hand to answer questions or give guidance as needed at such centers.

HELPING OTHER LEADERS

The church educational committee also needs to find or make training opportunities for helping leaders of other areas of work in the church understand and develop the educational potential of their work. This includes resource persons and other leaders whose primary work is not strictly education, but whose work communicates many of those unintentional learnings spoken of previously. Such leaders include the choir and junior choir directors, librarians, ushers, deacons and consistory, trustees, and other church leaders, especially the pastor. The education committee needs to point out to these people that their attitudes communicate; a personal impact or an impression of the church is made by their work and their relations with all other people; and that these contribute to the impact on all people in learning of what the church and faith are. Particularly with such persons as choir leaders it is important to emphasize the leadership aspect of their work and the affirmative contribution to worship, along with the educational opportunities for studying the meaning of what is sung. Such work is all part of the unplanned learning impact on the life of the congregation. While the board of education is not responsible for these persons and groups, it can work with them as partners in the learning and educational work of the church and its mission by offering and receiving ideas.

4. CHOOSE APPROPRIATE RESOURCES

"The first shall be last." Too often we have begun our thinking about planned Christian educational opportunities in the church, especially the school of the church, with the question: "What materials will we use?" As we have seen, however, there are prior questions: What is our church about? What is its mission? What are its basic theological and educational understandings? What are our goals or purposes for education? Who are the people of our church? What are their educational needs, and what abilities do they have to share? What unplanned learnings are influencing their understanding of God and the life and mission of Christian persons and the church? How shall we plan for our intentional teaching/learning programs? What settings are most appropriate for different kinds of educational events? What are our leadership needs and how can we recruit and train these leaders? What is our understanding of how persons learn?

When all these questions have been taken into consideration, *then* it is appropriate to ask: *"What resources shall we use?"*

Note that the inappropriate first question related to *materials* only. The appropriate final question used the broader term *resources*. Resources include people, environment, and all types of materials from art supplies through printed and audiovisual resources.

PEOPLE RESOURCES

Many people resources are needed in a wholistic educational program. The most important people resources, of course, are the leaders who are willing to commit their time and talent to work with particular groups for a given period of time or during a specified unit. The minister and other leaders also play significant roles. Through the sermon the minister helps members of the congregation understand the biblical message and the mission of Christians and the church in today's world. The organist and choir leader determine much of the educational impact of music in the life of the church. The church secretary is a key person in answering questions, keeping people informed, preparing needed resources and making all kinds of arrangements. The sexton can almost make or break an educational program through his/her attitude and approach to work around the church building and the people whom he or she encounters.

A good example of the role of the sexton can be seen in the contributions of Azor, a man well up in years. Azor not only kept the church building in good shape; he always appeared to be happy to see that everything was ready for every meeting. His temper never frayed, no matter how many times people changed their minds about what they wanted, or when. The children loved him and his special courtesy. Many adults benefited from a smile, a special word, or a personal favor from Azor. He ministered through everything he did and was.

Good administrators are needed for the educational ministry of the church. These may include a minister or director of Christian education, as well as members of the Christian education committee or board, church school and departmental superintendents, youth advisers, librarian, supply- and record-secretaries, and many others—including good cooks for those retreats and dinners! This listing may sound like a prescription for a large church, but it is not. The small church still needs people to perform these functions—even though some persons may do double duty!

All members of the church and community are potential resources for Christian education. These people have many skills and abilities needed for a good education program. Someone is especially good at storytelling. Another person is interested in children's books and can suggest books for the reading centers, or serve as a librarian. Still others may be called upon to share, at least briefly, their talents in carpentering, gardening, photography, knowledge of science, drama, music, writing, poster-making, other art skills, sewing, and the like. One church was conducting an adult series on "Church and State." Local judges, the mayor, the police chief, a county commissioner, a director of rehabilitation for the imprisoned were some of the resource persons called on to help people think about issues of church-state relationships.

Some resource people have a special skill in relating to persons of particular ages. Mrs. Nolen is just a garrulous elderly woman to many people; but to the infants, toddlers and children with whom she has worked in the church nursery, she is the most wonderful person in the world. She remembers their names and their birthdays and what they like. In the church coffee hour "her children" (of whatever age) flock around her. To them "being Christian" is being like Mrs. Nolen.

Mr. Toomey, on the other hand, does not relate well to younger children, but post-high-school youth and young adults in his church find rap sessions in his home most stimulating. "Mr. Toomey doesn't say very much, but you know he respects you, and he asks questions that really make you think." Because of these rap sessions, many participants have become actively involved in local political issues, especially in relation to the work of the school board and the city council.

Any local community is a hunting-and-finding ground for resources. Libraries, museums, theaters, special community celebrations, historic sites—all such places or events occurring in the community can be fed into the life of a congregation. So also can the many opportunities for service and mission, particularly carried out as two-way "streets" for insuring justice and a more humane world.

All resource people should be used effectively. They should not be expected to waste their time sitting through a lot of business unrelated to the task they have been asked to do. They should be thoroughly briefed in advance on what the groups are doing and how their contributions will fit into the ongoing process. Some people may elect to visit groups for an entire meeting or session; others may have time only to come in, make their presentation or other contribution, and leave. The groups likewise should be prepared to get the most from the participation of the resource persons by understanding ahead of time why the person is coming, and planning questions to be asked. If there are to be follow-up relationships, this element should be considered in advance.

ENVIRONMENT AND SUPPLIES
Too often the environment as a learning resource is overlooked. Pictures on the walls, tables and chairs arranged for work, equipment and supplies out and ready for use, books attractively arranged, learning centers set up and ready to go, all influence the learning potential in a positive way. On the other hand, a room with disarranged furnishings, scraps on the floor, dusty windowsills, books and papers haphazardly strewn on the table tells

persons that no one is particularly concerned with what is going to happen in that place or space.

When we walk into the sanctuary, the altar, the pulpit, the room arrangement, the windows (whether clear glass to let in the beauty of the world or stained glass with its beauty and symbols) all contribute to a sense of something important above and beyond ourselves. The environment prepares us for participating meaningfully in the service of worship, even as music sets the mood for worship.

Meeting rooms for educational activities, whether they be shared space or individual rooms, need to be learning environments. An Episcopal bishop once commented that our church schools are ersatz institutions. "Children and young people know what real schools are," he said. "They are places with chairs and tables and desks and chalkboards, books and pencils, pictures and other learning resources, and well-prepared teachers." If we want to reclaim church education, one of the things we must do is to work at developing and keeping up a learning environment, particularly in space for planned educational events.

It is not necessary, or even desirable, for leaders to do all the preparation of the learning environment. In the church school, students should be involved in deciding how the room or space should be arranged, in selecting pictures, in decorating the bulletin board or wall space, in being responsible for cleaning up and setting up the room or area. Such involvement increases learnings about responsibility and self-worth ("I am important in this group") and increases interest in the life and work of the group.

If your church has a room or corner designated especially for youth activities, the young people should be responsible for setup and decor (after clearing with persons responsible for maintenance of the building). One church that used an old parsonage as an educational activity building, turned the basement over to the teenagers. Walls were painted in gay bright colors; posters were put on; a strobe light and cushions were furnished, along with tables and chairs. Putting it all together was a glorious time for the young people—and they learned a lot about practical matters and human relationships.

Supplies for various groups should be kept where they are easily accessible to the users. Someone other than teachers should be responsible for gathering and keeping basic supplies of paper, pencils, paint, paste, scissors, clay, and the like. This is a task for a volunteer (a resource person) who does not wish to assume a teaching job but who is willing to spend an hour or so a week finding out what is needed, to replace supplies used up, and to keep the supply cupboards or closets neatly organized. For a large church, a committee of several persons may be used for this task.

Books, pictures, filmstrips, slides, records, tapes, and audiovisual equipment also require a person or group of persons to keep them available and in working order. These resources are usually the responsibility of a media-librarian or committee.

A media center or library is an important resource, whether it be a few shelves and a table in a corner or hallway, or a room set aside for this purpose. It provides resources for all types of planned educational programs. It also provides learning resources for persons not participating in planned programs. The librarian in one small church media center renders a real ministry by taking or sending books and records to shut-ins. Tapes of the minister's sermons can also be made available to those unable to be present at a worship service.

Most churches have more supplies and equipment than they realize. If more are needed, they can be increased at little cost. The first step is to go through every classroom, every closet, every cupboard, every bookcase, any place items might be stored. Make a catalog card for each permanent item. This would include a card for each teaching picture, but not for unmounted pictures from magazines that are for use in art projects. The name, subject area, kind of resource, and where it is stored should be entered on each card. Someone who wants resources on saints would then look in the card catalog under "saints" to discover that there is a picture of St. Francis hanging in the back of the sanctuary, a filmstrip, several books and pictures of saints in the media center. Any of these can be borrowed by signing a take-out card.

In like manner, find out what items are needed and have an adequate supply on hand. Replenish *before* the supply is gone. Many used items can be recycled. When small bottles of paste or glue are empty, the dry residue can be cleaned out and the bottles refilled from an economical large-size bottle. Paper may be removed from broken crayons so they can be used to make broad bands of color by using the sides rather than the ends. (To keep these crayons from picking up color from one another, sort them by color in egg cartons.) It is not necessary to have unused newsprint for making charts. Newspaper pages that do not have large blocks of heavy type can be written on with a broad-tipped marker or bright crayon.

Be resourceful. Usable cupboards for classroom storage can be made by gluing together several sturdy cartons picked up at stores. These can be made even more durable by covering them inside and out with papier-mache. To make them attractive, paint or cover with wallpaper or make a collage of pictures cut from magazines.

Keeping supplies and resources ready and in good condition takes time, but it pays off in easing the task of leaders and increasing the possibilities for learning. The more effective the resourcing staff, the more effective teaching/learning is apt to be.

CURRICULAR RESOURCES FOR PLANNED EDUCATION

Well-planned and prepared units of study are important resources for all educators, but especially for volunteer leaders who have had little training in Bible, theology, and educational methodology. Good curriculum resources are written by people with excellent background in Bible, theology and the subject area, plus knowledge and experience in teaching/learning techniques for the particular age groups for which the materials are prepared. These resources provide helps and guidance for teachers, and at the same time are open enough for teachers to adapt the material to the particular concerns and abilities of their students.

Not-so-good curricular resources usually pay less attention to individual differences in interests, needs, and abilities of learners. The typical "lesson" unit usually starts with a Bible verse, then has a story or other material to be read or told, followed by questions about the content. The questions may be in a variety of forms: crossword puzzles, filling in blanks, matching statements or words, or verbal responses. For younger age groups there usually are some kind of art activities more or less related to the "lesson": pictures to be colored, figures to be cut out and mounted, and the like. Little attention is given to creativity or to questions and problems raised by the students. Only the story, Bible verse, and questions are considered learning opportunities. Personal and group relationships, use of skills to create or to work cooperatively, and opportunities to engage in mission are overlooked in assessing learning.

Let us hasten to say that using stories and other materials and answering questions about the content are good teaching/ learning techniques, but they need to be balanced with more involving methods related to "discovery learning" that help the learners explore feelings, ideas, and information in a variety of ways. Discovery learning techniques include dramatic playing out of problems; developing art projects that help students conceptualize ideas; using games, action projects, research, simulations, open discussion and the like. And we must never forget that attitudes and environment may teach more than all our words put together. Ignoring a student, frowning harshly, may blot out verses and statements about God's love.

In wholistic education, the selection of resources is made by the education committee or other group charged with this responsibility. This group is aware of the goals for Christian education and the theological and educational stances of the church. It looks for resources that will help persons move toward these goals and be in keeping with the general point of view of the church.

The best place to start looking is usually with curricula recommended by denominational education specialists. These curricula are designed from a theological point of view in keeping with the creeds or statements of faith adopted by the denomination. The educational stance emphasizes the priorities of the denomination, and the resources are prepared with the abilities and needs of the majority of the churches of that denomination in mind.

Currently a dozen or more denominations have banded together to prepare resources for four approaches to meet a broad spectrum of concerns and needs of different churches in each of the denominations. These approaches, prepared by JED (Joint Educational Development), are called "Christian Education: Shared Approaches." All four approaches share a common, basic theological and educational stance but have individual goals and approaches as follows:

1. *KNOWING THE WORD* RESOURCES. The goal of this approach is to enable persons to know the contents of the Bible and to respond as faithful disciples. The materials are designed to have each session start with a portion of scripture which is then related to the life of the students. This approach generally requires less preparation time for the teachers as it relies more heavily on a deductive than inductive educational approach.

2. *INTERPRETING THE WORD* RESOURCES. This approach again starts with scripture for the purpose of enabling persons to increase their ability to respond to the Bible and to be able to interpret the scriptures informatively. Time and effort is spent on the exegesis of the biblical material to help students increase their knowledge of the background and interpretation of the biblical message.

3. *LIVING THE WORD* RESOURCES. This third approach sometimes starts with biblical material, sometimes with current concerns. Its emphasis is upon living out the biblical message in the church, the community and the world. Its goal is to enable persons to participate in the life and mission of the church as disciples of Jesus Christ. It views the life of the church community as the teaching/learning context.

4. *DOING THE WORD* RESOURCES. As the name implies, this approach emphasizes an action/reflection mode of learning, starting with either the biblical message or the mission of God in the world to put Christ's teachings into action. The goal of this approach is to engage persons actively in the Christian mission at home and abroad.

In addition, three JED planning guides have been designed to help local churches decide which approach or what combination of approaches might be best for an individual church. The guides vary according to how much time and effort the local church wants to put in making these decisions. *Developing the Congregation's Educational Program* gives a fairly detailed description of each of the approaches, and step-by-step guidance for developing a congregation's own program. A committee may expect to need ten hours for use of this guide. *Planning for Education in the Congregation* is a multimedia kit with resources for involving the planners in theological, educational, and resource dimensions of the planning process. Gathering information, planning, and making decisions takes a minimum of twelve hours. *Creating the Congregation's Educational Ministry* is an ambitious program that moves a congregation from the creation of a statement of its mission to the development and evaluation of its educational program. This two-volume guide assumes a study of several months' duration.

Most widely used curricula do not have as much guidance materials as "Christian Education: Shared Approaches," but they do have some kind of guide or brochure that tells about the content and approaches to education and theology. The first step for a committee, therefore, is to write to denominational headquarters or commercial companies for such overviews of the curricula. (When we speak of commercial curricula, we are referring to non-denominational publishing houses that produce church school curricula on a commercial, profit-making basis.)

When the committee has narrowed its choices on the basis of reading the brochures or planning guides, it is ready to order a sample set of the resources. Things to look for in the materials include:

1. What do the introductions in the leaders' guides say about the approach to the Bible with the particular age group?
2. What is the general theological point of view found in the introductions and in a sampling of stories or other content?
3. What do the introductions say about the educational point of view? If the introduction is not clear, browse through the teaching suggestions for the types of learning activities suggested. Are they discovery-type activities or verbal responses plus outlined "busywork"?
4. Are there suggestions for setting goals and objectives and ways to evaluate sessions, units and courses?
5. Are the materials attractive and inviting to use?
6. Is there a good variety of resources—pictures, records or tapes, filmstrips and suggestions of additional resources, or are the materials dependent upon the printed word only?
7. Do the materials incorporate a whole-church point of view or treat church school as a separate entity?

Seldom if ever will a given set of curriculum resources meet exactly the needs and concerns of a congregation or a particular group. The materials have to be adapted, enriched with additional resources, shortened or lengthened according to time and interest. Selecting and using resources is like trying to buy a ready-made garment for a person who is hard to fit. It has to be taken in, let out, adjusted here and there, and appropriate accessories have to be added to complete the appearance. When this is done carefully, the outcome is well worth the time and expense.

5. PUT IT ALL TOGETHER

In this book we have been examining essential components of an educational program developed from the wholistic point of view.

Components are ingredients that can be put together in a variety of ways. Thus far we have considered these components:
- the nature of the wholistic approach to Christian education;
- the four elements that make up the "whole" in an educational ministry: people in church and community; the heritage of the faith; mission; the life of the congregation;
- identifying what the congregation believes about theology;
- identifying what we believe about education, how people learn, who teachers are, and what teaching is;
- knowing the people, their interests, needs and concerns;
- deciding who is responsible for envisioning, developing, and carrying out the program;
- who make desirable leaders, and how we select and train them;
- choosing appropriate resources.

Now we come to the point of putting all these components together. This means planning ways and programs to accomplish our purposes.

STARTING POINTS
As your committee or board of education has thought about the components, you have probably worked on what you want Christian education to accomplish. Goals and specific objectives for the year ahead in the church's educational ministry may have been decided. Perhaps you have already begun to pinpoint the best places where planned education can be effective, and have also noted some of the occasions in the church's life where unplanned or by-product learnings occur. One way of beginning to work on the wholistic perspective is to talk with other boards, such as deacons or consistories or trustees or youth groups, about ways that the Christian education committee and these organizations or groups can think and work to bring planned and unplanned learning into consideration in the educational ministry.

Where do we begin? This inquiry indicates a search for a starting point in terms of event or special opportunity, a specific point of entry, especially one that will help to illustrate the wholistic approach that undergirds the total educational ministry. One important specific possibility is to take a situation where education is not going well and try to transform it. Or, a situation where planned and unplanned learning opportunities are on a collision course. As an example of the latter, one large church needed a big, open room as a location for the opening and closing sessions of its learning center for children. The only such room was occupied by the choir for rehearsals for thirty minutes before the second worship service of the morning and was declared unavailable to the church school, even though learning center sessions were held during both morning services of worship. Obviously, the fine art of church political negotiation was involved. Even more basically, a thorough survey of facilities was needed with consultations among educational leaders, choir directors and organist, trustees, the pastor and many other persons. It was decided to hold a special meeting of all those involved in boards and other groups within the church in order to make an evaluative survey of all the programs and their leadership.

The total wholistic approach to education was presented, including the important contributions to unplanned learning made by the choir on Sundays and in other musical services. It took a weekend retreat of honest, often fiery discussion, for the problem which began the whole discussion to be solved. The trustees discovered that certain temporary walls could be knocked out to provide choir rehearsal space that would be adequate. This left the other room, which was adjacent to the smaller rooms also used in the learning center groups, available for that educational special event.

A further result of this point of beginning with a difficult problem was greater all-round understanding of wholistic educational ministry, and the discovery of some ways in which the choir and junior choir and educational events could develop mutual relationships and sharing.

In another church, the church school was going downhill. A careful evaluation suggested that a learning center approach be tried for a year. The program was carefully planned, and this approach went along for a year. The church school numbered three hundred and met in two sessions, simultaneously with the church services. First stages had been great. Monthly themes were used to form the focal points for activities and study. The purpose had been to involve church and church school in a common emphasis. In October, on Worldwide Communion Sunday, several weeks of advance preparation resulted in the church school making a huge wall poster-board showing the communion elements with the legend "Thanks be to God." It was presented to the congregation during the worship service as a permanent wall hanging in the educational wing of the church building.

As the year went on, however, something began to slip. Activities became stressed more than the substance which was expressed through those activities. Complaints from parents about "no Bible" began to arise, so an optional unit that utilized the denominational curriculum as resource was included in the learning center offerings. There seemed to be less relationship between church and church school.

At year's end, evaluation by the board of Christian education meeting with the pastor concluded thatt, despite careful weekly leader preparation, numbers were too great, and other factors were stumbling blocks to continuing the learning center as such. The goal of a wholistic approach had not really been achieved. But the desire for forms of education to meet the interests of the people and involve the mission and faith commitments of the congregation continued. A new design for the church school featured combined study and activity for the children. Seminars for youth and adults were added, and a series of quarterly retreats was planned for the whole church for fellowship and intensive examination of selected issues in mission to the world. Deacons launched a study of the church's policy regarding the sacraments, prepared a statement on baptism, and brought this to the congregation for discussion and decision.

Thus in this church, an experiment starting with the church school proved unsatisfactory, even though it led to rethinking and revision and then expansion into broader age groupings and more participation by other church groups in educational program. This church continues this open-ended kind of evaluation and designing of additional opportunities as needs and interests indicate, but it is still working toward the goal of a wholistic involvement. Taking into account unplanned learning opportunities is only beginning to get under way.

By contrast, in another part of the country, a small church in a metropolitan suburb (the suburb is older than the city!) began to plan from a wholistic perspective under entirely different circumstances. Analysis of its church membership showed only a few couples with preschool or elementary age children, a dozen or so youth, and a good many couples fortyish and up in age. In this community, many patterns of family life were widely accepted. The traditional Sunday school in the church, no matter what the format, just did not go—people did not attend. Examination of the congregation's theological and educational assumptions suggested considerable diversity in theology, but a strong desire for freer forms of education that would give opportunity for some intergenerational sessions for a while, then broad age groupings—an arrangement that would be conducive to freedom of expression coupled with some input about Christian faith and today's problems.

To begin its redesigning, this church called together a committee on education composed of representatives of various church organizations, with the minister as the enabler-leader for the time being. Family cluster sessions on such issues as "Jesus," "World Hunger and the Christian," "Family Life Today," "Technology and Values" were listed. Some groups were to meet on Sunday morning; others were to gather in retreats. Attention was also given to ways of making the Sunday morning service one of worship and celebration in which all ages could participate. The committee on education planned to study the congregational life for other opportunities, and also to find out more about recruiting new participants from the community who did not feel at home in either of the other two churches located there, but who might respond favorably to the developing style of program being designed.

Each of these very different churches is using the components of the wholistic perspective. Because this is so, the resulting programs are very different. One has encountered more difficulties in planning than the other. In each case, however, the people have felt confidence in their ability to work out their program designs. A few people with intense interest and commitment have sparked the cause of the wholistic approach to education, and have enlisted other interested workers whose dedication has increased. Regular meetings for planning and evaluation have been essential to development of the program—and those planning sessions, according to the people involved, have provided great personal enrichment. Why not? they say. The work of planning keeps the Christian heritage, people, the mission, the congregation, and people's interests before the committee, sparks the committee's own thinking and personal growth, and arouses excitement about its work.

NO SINGLE PATTERN
No single pattern can be prescribed for education developed from a wholistic perspective. Illustrations and reports already

mentioned in earlier chapters of this book testify to the rich variety that results from tailoring Christian education in the manner we have been discussing.

Some leaders who have dipped their toes into the waters of developing education from a whole-church perspective have found widespread, hearty and enthusiastic response. Others have found that response has been more limited and that adults are reluctant to change established patterns, but these leaders have gone ahead with those who have responded. Whatever the response may be, work with those who will be worked with! And persevere quietly but firmly. A slow start on a new approach to educational ministry is by no means unusual.

In some instances committees proceed with only nominal pastoral support. Many ministers are not trained in education, and are accustomed to leaving that work to church members. But even the busiest of non-educationally trained pastors have become involved when a few satisfying experiences in hitherto unplowed educational ground in the church are favorably received. The minister is especially well qualified to serve as biblical and theological adviser and group leader. Confirmation is also a particular interest of pastors. In a number of churches, concern for confirmation training has served as an avenue for mutual relationships between committee and pastor in the interest of the Christian education of the church's young people.

However you arrange and plan to use the components of the wholistic approach in developing your program of educational ministries, putting it all together can be a stimulating, creative, sometimes frustrating, but ultimately rewarding venture. The starting point may be an educational venture that isn't working, or it may be a visible need that cries out to be fulfilled. The process of designing program built on the components can become a genuinely wholistic approach that gradually involves all the congregation in learning and experiencing the faith and acting upon it in mission.

ONE POSSIBLE PROCESS FOR PUTTING IT ALL TOGETHER

SEVEN STEPS IN EDUCATIONAL PLANNING

Basic steps in what is called "the planning process" are very similar, regardless of the different titles that may be given to the steps by various specialists. Here are seven steps in educational planning in the local church which have been used and tested in a number of church educational leadership workshops. The steps are one good sequence of what to do in the process of putting the components of a Christian education ministry together in wholistic fashion. They were designed by Carl Bade.

STEP ONE. *Explore or define the existing or hoped for program.* (Refer to Chapter 4, section 1 [pages 27-41] and Chapter 5, sections 1 and 3 [pages 89-92 and 99-104].)

Two ways of doing this step are by "Analysis" and by "Futuring." Either way may be used individually. Utilizing both together would be most effective.

Analysis consists of the following:
- Data Gathering
- Situation Analysis
- Issue Definition
- Problem Definition
- Identifying the Concerns

Analysis may include developing a membership profile; developing a common understanding of the community; reviewing the current educational problems of the church (strong programs, weak programs, gaps); understanding clearly the organizational arrangement; reviewing the financial resources; determining available leadership; determining the climate that prevails in the congregation.

Futuring requires these steps:
Assume no restraint on numbers of persons, materials, equipment and finances; then create your dream of an education program for the congregation for any (or all) of these periods of time:
- 10 years from now
- 5 years from now
- 1 year from now

STEP TWO. *(a) Develop theological foundations or assumptions of the congregation.*

(b) Develop educational foundations or assumptions of the congregation (For theological foundation refer to Chapter 4, section 2 [pages 41-54], and to Chapter 3 [pages 17-25]; for educational assumptions refer to Chapter 4, section 3 [pages 54-87], and to Chapter 2 [pages 11-15.])

STEP THREE. *Set the Goal(s).* A goal is a broad, long range purpose, without detailed content or time limit. (Refer to Chapter 4, section 1 [pages 27-41].)

STEP FOUR. *Set Objectives.* An objective is a statement of desired outcome in measurable terms. (Refer to Chapter 4, section 3 [pages 54-87].)

STEP FIVE. *Review the Resources:* persons, facilities, materials, financing. (Refer to Chapter 5, section 4 [pages 104-12].)

STEP SIX. *Develop and Implement Your Educational Program.* (Refer to Chapter 5 [pages 89-119].)

STEP SEVEN. *Evaluate Your Work:*
- as you move along;
- when a period of time is complete;
- the results of any portion of, or the total, program.

(Refer to Chapter 6 [pages 121-22].)

SPECIAL NOTE. Planning is not one-way—once you have completed one step, don't think it can be forgotten. As you move through the entire process, you will need to refer to completed steps many times. For example, choosing resources will be decided on the basis of goals, and theological and educational foundations. Or, selection of goals and objectives will depend on results of exploring your present situation and theological and educational foundations. Implementing the program will rely on what you have discovered in doing all the preceding steps. So it goes. Planning is dynamic. In it, you will make use of every piece of work you have done! That's why planning wholistic educational ministries helps to bring people and churches alive and provide renewed vitality.

CHAPTER 6

KEEPING EDUCATION FRESH AND ALIVE

Pages could be written on the question of keeping education fresh and alive in the church. Perhaps the pages you have already read in this book will offer some answers.

A process, however, should be set up for this express purpose. Having planned a total program for a period of time—whether three months, six months, or a year—do not think that this is the program for all time. Check and change as needed for every block of time, and every portion of the program.

Evaluation is the term commonly used for this process. The board of Christian education may take primary responsibility. Participants in program units may be given a chance to rate the units. Sometimes a rating scale of five numbers ranging from "Not at all satisfactory" 1..2..3..4..5 "Very satisfactory" may be used, with chance to write in specific comments and suggestions. This type of evaluation is more suitable for youth or adults. Children may be interviewed informally: "What did you like best of what you've been doing?" "Do you like to do one kind of thing (specific example) more than others?" "What would interest you next time?" or "in the future?"

Evaluation comments need to be taken seriously, but not as the only way of checking. Attendance may be another criterion—provided the attendance pattern of the entire congregation is included in the study, along with community customs for weekending, or business and community involvements during the weektime. The latter inevitably affect church attendance. So also do Saturday night activities, distance from the church, degree of interest of adults in helping children get to church, and many other similar factors.

Keeping in touch with church members, especially participants in the educational program, by informal conversation or by "sounding questionnaires" (once in a while) is an invaluable and reliable way of finding out what concerns people, and what might effectively be dealt with at a future time, or immediately in designing program.

In addition, regular planning/evaluation sessions are indispensable. A team of five members and their pastor from a small church in the Great Plains section of our country attended a workshop on wholistic approach. Members of the team represented church school, board of education, lay-fellowship groups, the trustees, and youth. On their return they pursued many of the steps already suggested in this book. The program that they developed touched every part of the church's life. The simple arrangement of their church building lent itself to being easily changed for educational groups, worship, and all-church events. New life flourished in the church. How was it kept fresh and alive? By the fact that the teams met regularly (at 6:45 A.M. on Mondays, for breakfast, before members went to work!) to evaluate and make decisions that would enable the educational ministry to involve everyone some way.

Teaching . . . learning . . . thinking theologically . . . exercising leadership: all are processes that must ebb and flow as ocean waves do. None of them can be put into a formula and be allowed to run on without examination, constructive criticism, keeping a weather eye out for what's happening, and then having the courage and commitment to make changes that enhance and enrich the educational ministries from a wholistic perspective. Lots of work? Probably. But done in the spirit of helping a Christian congregation fulfill its mission in a day that cries out for religious and moral guidance, reclaiming Christian education by this wholistic approach is an enterprise worthy of such commitment. It is an essential ministry of the whole church.